Chariots of Fire:

A Tibetan

Historical

Perspective

Kevin Kieswetter

Table of Contents

PREFACE

Washington DC based Pew Research Center found in 2010 that 18.2% of Chinese are followers of Buddhism, while, a similar study at Purdue University yielded a similar result.[1] Suffice it to say, there are many Chinese who are adherents of other religions or are agnostic. These numbers reflect a large cleavage to be influenced through state-fuelled propaganda, advertising, and other media.

The essence of this paper is to begin from the beginning for Tibet. As can be expected, there is a shortage of works that date back to its inception, however, many scholars will agree that Tibet was founded on spirituality and agrarian muscle. Comparisons are drawn between the Chinese modelof Buddhism versus Tibet's, that is, the sudden awakening of the mind/body/spirit compared to a gradualist approach, respectively.

The central argument here rests on China's claim to Tibet and their occupation. This is where I wholeheartedly disagree and spend the basis of my research refuting. Recent history will show that the international community, though still gaining cohesion after the close of WWII, failed to respond to China's occupation and annexation of Tibet in 1949. China, as a voting member of the P5 – United Nations- can veto any sanctions proposed against it. China, perhaps sensing an opportunity within Tibet, moved slowly at first, though found traction on the premise that modernisation of the feudal system was necessary to bolster the economy and improve living conditions. As the occupation continued throughout the 1950's, religious rights and freedoms began to diminish.

---

[1] Wikipedia. "Religion in China; 3.1 Statistics." 15 March 2014. 20 March 2014. <http://www.en.wikipedia.org/wiki/Religion_in_China>.

Finally, in 1959 after a failed coup by Tibetans against their Chinese occupiers, the Dalai Lama fled to India to establish a government – in – exile. Without a strong central figure in Tibet to mitigate against increasingly oppressive conditions, Warren Smith best sums up the situation that "... during the Cultural Revolution (1966-1971), there was not even the pretense of respect for Tibetan autonomy." [2] The situation on the ground continued to be problematic for Tibetans beyond 1976. Despite Mao's death in 1976 and his a priori selection of the moderate, Hua Guofeng, the situation remains bleak for Tibetans. The Dalai Lama remains in exile in India, though a new political leader – Dr. Lobsang Sangay was installed in 2011 as the third democratically elected 'Kalon Tripa' or executive of the TGIE, thus, leaving the Dalai Lama to attend to spiritual matters. China's constitution, particularly, Article 10, authorises the state to expropriate land in the public interest. This has hindered the notion of property rights for Chinese citizens. [3] Confidence in China's ruling elites has remained dubious with state-centered political decisions that delay much needed reforms, corruption among public officials, too much emphasis on private enterprise, labour unrest, and the magnitude of pollution and associated health problems. These issues have given rise to discontent as evidenced by the escalation of civil disobedience that number upwards of 80,000 incidents on an annual basis.

---

[2] Smith Jr., Warren W. China's Tibet. New York: Rowman & Littlefield Publishers Inc., 2008, xv1. Mao Zedong was seeking a way to reform China from its bourgeoisie past through a system of 'Red Guards' who acted as spies against public officials who were unwilling to break from past tendencies, and eliminate those with capitalist ambitions. Unfortunately, for Tibetans many Buddhist temples were destroyed along with sacred texts.

[3] Lieberthal, Kenneth. Governing China From Revolution Through Reform. New York: W.W. Norton & Co., 2004.

Map of Tibet and surrounding area: Bhutan, Sikkim, Nepal, and Xinjiang. Used with kind permission from the British Library

THOG MA NAS "FROM THE BEGINNING"

The monastic community in Tibet continues to be at odds with China's austere policies regarding adherents of Buddhism. Since 2008, Chinese officials in Tibet have incarcerated 731 political prisoners, of which, 261 are monks and 116 are nuns.[4]

Tibet is known as the "rooftop" of the world with its thin air, arid land, scenic mountaintops, and dedication to the Buddhist culture and beliefs. Tibetan Buddhism, according to scholars, was found during the period of the "Religious Kings; in particular, during the reign of Songtsen Gampo (c. 618-650). Avalokitesvara, the Buddha of compassion is considered to be an incarnate of the "Three Kings" and a "founding" spiritual presence in Tibet dating to the Yarlung Dynasty around 233 C.E. Thus, Songtsen Gampo had two missions: to spread the dharma and Buddhism, and consolidate a powerful political base in Lhasa for Tibet in Central Asia, which he did successfully. In fact, a palace was built-the Potala-which was the official residence of the Dalai Lamas preceding the annexation by China in 1959.[5]

Tibet has endured considerable strain due to the Chinese occupation, both to its "natural" citizens and habitat. China has a spotty record on human rights domestically, which has manifest in Tibet. The incursion of Han Chinese has left natural Tibetans, as subordinate to the Han Chinese; in particular, in Lhasa where they number approximately 200,000 households compared to 150,000 Tibetan households. A considerable portion of Han

---

[4] International Campaign For Tibet. Website Content Producer, Morgan Riehl.9 April 2014.<http://www.savetibet.org/wpcontent/uploads/2013/06/ICT_political_priso ner_list_full.pdf >.
[5] Powers, John. Introduction to Tibetan Buddhism. New York: Snow Lion Publications, 2007, 144.

émigré's correlate to the development of the Qinghai-Lhasa railway that has spawned the influx of Han for construction. The railway began operations in 2006 connecting Lhasa to Beijing. Tibetans, despite their spirited resistance are generally magnanimous towards their Chinese occupiers, due in large part to their grounding in Buddhism and duty to The Dalai Lama, who promotes peace and tolerance towards all sentient beings. Invariably, a sense of apathy is apparent due to the protracted nature of the occupation and coercive tactics employed by Chinese officials. The continuing incidents of self-immolations cannot be "explained away" solely through fear and hopelessness. Isolation from democratised nations plays a huge role in fostering outbreaks against Chinese officials, and isolated incidents against Han Chinese business owners during the Beijing Summer Olympics.

The object of this paper seeks solutions to the Chinese occupation of Tibet through historical evidence, religious and cultural distinctions, and Tibet's position via the TGIE (Tibetan Government In Exile). The notion of human rights will bring into focus China's record, particularly prior to and during the 2008 Olympic games in Beijing. Can the International Community play a positive role in aiding Tibetans to form a working partnership with China, do economic sanctions promoted through individual state initiatives encourage repercussions, or does a boycott of Chinese consumer goods provide a viable solution to resolving the impasse? What are ways in which the Tibetan Diaspora and supporters can influence the Chinese response towards holding meaningful talks to narrow the cleavages? Moreover, inclusive in any future settlement should be the return to Tibet of the religious rights and freedoms to choose the successors to The Dalai Lama, Panchen Lama, and the TGIE.

Authors that lend defense to this perspective include: Melvyn Gldstein, Michael Davis, John Powers, Robert Thurman, and Donald S. Lopez.

Tibet has gradually been evolving from an underwater vestige of mountains and land as part of India that impacted with Asia almost forty million years ago. The shifting land mass forced the land upwards from the seabed to enable the formation of the Himalayas and the Tibetan plateau, as it is presently known.[6]

Its inhabitants refer to Tibet as "Pö" (bod). The origin of this name is uncertain, but may have originally meant "native land" or "original place." According to the Blue Annals (history of the Tibetan Buddhist lineages), it is a shortened form of the earlier name "Bugyel" (spu rgyal), but the White Annals[7] contends that it is derived from the pre-Buddhist religion of Bön (bon). The name "Tibet," by which it is known to the outside world, is probably derived from the Mongolian word "Thubet." It is often called "Kangchen" (Gangs can) by its inhabitants, meaning "Land of Snows."[8] Thus, Tibetan lineage encompassing language, religion and geography dates many centuries ago and illustrates the strength of Buddhism as a central force within the country, that has allowed for it's development and autonomy at it's inception. Indeed, the 'Blue Annals' are analogous to the "First Testament" of Christianity teachings in terms of the period and structure vis- à- vis prayers and ideology.

---

[6] Powers, 140.

[7] Lopez, Donald S. The Madman's Middle Way. Chicago and London: The University of Chicago Press, 2006, 13, 30. 'The White Annals' are works on the early history of Tibet around the period of the Yarlung Dynasty as written by Gendun Chopel and a response to the 'Blue Annals,' a prodigious volume composed in 1476 regarding the history of Tibetan Buddhist lineages.

[8] Powers, John. 137.

Since the invasion and occupation of Tibet by China, there has been a program of assimilation inside Tibet to inculcate present and future generations of Tibetans and Han Chinese to encompass Chinese thought and culture. Textbooks, newspapers, television and all forms of media are rigorously produced and consumed with 'selling the notion of Tibetan historical autonomy' as farcical. Some scholars accept these claims, while defending the Tibetan occupation in positive terms backed up with data from the Peoples Republic of China (PRC), regarding financial expenditures such as … 95% of the 10.6 billion between 1965-2004 for the Tibet Autonomous Region (TAR) and 4.4 billion on infrastructure projects.[9] Unfortunately, the nature of this data is difficult to corroborate owing to the inclusive nature of China's information within its borders and to the International Community. The expanse of corruption among public officials impacts any transparency of information available to its citizens, NGO's or the International Community.

The influence of Tibetan lineage has had a major impact in the eastern Sino-Tibetan region that pre-dates the Yarlung Dynasty. The genesis of Tibetan ancestral roots is associated with the Qiang where similar traits were found linguistically. To bolster the notion of Tibetan suzerainty during this period, noted Tibetologist, R.A. Stein infers that these two groups are not identical, though the Tibetans are one of the principal elements, which contributed to the Qiang formation.[10] Qiang hegemony may have been reported in historical records that indicated domination over the culture of early Tibet; it is viewed

---

[9] Sautman, Barry (2006)'Colonialism, genocide, and Tibet', Asian Ethnicity, 7:3,243 — 265

[10] Smith Jr, Warren W. China's Tibet. Lanham: Rowman & Littlefield Publishers, 2008,2.

that the Qiang exercised control over artifacts and the indigenous people's traditions that resulted in little evidence remaining to expose the Qiang as immigrants.[11] It is analogous to the current trend that demonstrates the assimilation of Han Chinese into Tibet to instill Chinese sovereignty, both economically and culturally.

A unified Tibet estimated around 600-630, though nascent politically, found strength and order during the Yarlung Dynasty through a society and political institution that was a "feudal confederation of tribes." The clan structure was founded on a reward system to leverage political cooperation and loyalty.[12]

While the Yarlung Dynasty was consolidating power, Buddhism was emerging as the preeminent religion in Tibet, while dispersing through to Central Asia, India and along trade routes, including China where several cities were under Chinese control. John Powers describes the irony in which "Tibet first came into contact with the religion as an invading force that ransacked Buddhist institutions in Central Asia and put many monks to death during its military incursions." The next several centuries, despite the destruction of Buddhist temples and violence toward its adherents saw the manifestation of Buddhism in Tibetans, who became passionate supporters of the dharma.[13]

Tibet's military strength made it a regional power that culminated with an attack on China, enabling it to capture substantial areas of land that China held jurisdiction over. These areas included four principal Chinese bastions in Turkistan that concluded with the forfeiture of Chinese communication with the west. In addition, the Tibetan dynasty

---

[11] Smith Jr, 2.
[12] Smith Jr, 3.
[13] Powers, 142-143.

would capture "all of Gansu, and most of Szechwan and northern Yunnan." Moreover, an annual tribute was required of the Chinese emperor as payment to the Yarlung kings. In 763 after failure to make the payment, the Tibetans assaulted, captured and razed Chagan- the Chinese capital. Tibetan and Chinese records indicate that both China and Tibet were major powers that enjoyed equal authority diplomatically, while Tibet was superior militarily.[14] Tibet and China were often at war leading up to 822 that brought both sides into a peaceful existence with the signing of a treaty that clarified Tibet and China as distinct and separate, with a demarcation line. As noted by Smith regarding the wording of the treaty, "All to the east of the boundary is the domain of Great China. All to the west is surely the domain of Great Tibet. In addition, the treaty said that "Tibetans shall be happy in the land of Tibet and Chinese shall be happy in the land of China."[15] Buddhist religion was the foundation of culture, and existence for Tibetans that remained relatively unchallenged leading up to, and during the period of the religious kings. However, there was controversy over the process of the Buddhist covenant - "awakening"; the purpose of practicing Buddhism is to purify "ones" spirit from negative past deeds in ones past lives and current life. The Indian process which was exported to Tibet is founded on the Mahayana tradition whose doctrine states that 'awakening' is a gradual process that may or may not be fulfilled in ones present life. In general, the process of attaining enlightenment is to practise the "Three Jewels"[1] "The Buddha" – the belief in Buddhism as an expression to understanding ones ultimate nature,[2] the dharma

---

[14] Powers, 143.
Chinese historians refute these claims of China paying Tibet an annual fee, however, Tang transcripts indicate, otherwise.
[15] Smith Jr, 5.

which is to teach and practise moral goodness, forgiveness, and non-violence, [3] and the sangha – involvement in the community of Buddhist monks and nuns.[16]

In particular, Buddhism advocates five spiritual paths to achieve enlightenment:

1) The Path of Accumulation

One garners merit by a display of honourable and moral deeds that create and "produce good karmic results and positive mental states." Wisdom is developed for the benefit of all sentient beings.

2) The Path of Preparation

Meditation is the vehicle to achieve this path when a level of inner calm with higher insight creates emptiness or the feeling of "suchness" which lead to the goal of reaching "the true nature of reality."

3) The Path of Seeing

Meditation is the means to bring about the absence of subject and object to manifest emptiness. Bodhisattvas (a person who achieves enlightenment for the benefit of other beings) experience emptiness beyond the mindfulness of worldly thought and mundane experiences.

4) The Path of Meditation

A person clears the exaggerated and/or undeveloped thoughts, however, subtle traces still exist in memory. The meditator experiences periods of uninterrupted paths that contain subtle impressions and the proceeding paths of liberation exposes clarity from these impressions.

---

[16] Powers, 522-526. These are included in the "Lexicon of Works" and are remedial, however, illustrate the process of practicing Buddhism while the five "Spiritual Paths" are more specific in describing personal requirements.

5) The Path of No More Learning

Meditators remove any remaining impressions along with any parts of their source. Bodhisattvas eliminate all impressions related to negative awareness due to previous incarnations and present existence, while attaining their desire to reach Buddhahood for the welfare of all sentient beings.[17]

In contrast, the Chinese Chan School (Zen) favour a process of "sudden awakening" in which one can attain Buddhahood, rapidly. These contrasting lineages set the stage for a historical debate at Lhasa around 792 – 794 ce. Heshang Moheyan), who was a proficient meditator, and monk, represented the Chinese (Chan) side. Kamala´sîla represented the Indic (Mahãyãna) side and was a student in India of ´Sântarakshita, who was acknowledged in Tibet as the "Bodhisattva Abbot," or a teacher for the benefit of others.[18] Legend states that Kamala´sîla was the victor of the debate resulting in Mahâyâna being the dominant Buddhist lineage recognised by the king, while Chan (Zen) was prohibited in Tibet. Legend indicates that upon leaving Tibet, Heshang left one shoe behind signifying that remnants of his opposing views. This metaphor has been characterized in present time in the manner of the People's Liberation Army and its mandate in Lhasa, the presence of karma, notwithstanding.[19] China and Tibet had acrimonious relations leading up to the debate, however given the Tibetan venue and king, an opposing verdict may have resulted in internal strife, despite the popularity of both streams of thought. The victory solidified Buddhist thought in Tibet and would sustain Tibet after the collapse of the Tibetan Empire in 842. According to Smith Tibet

---

[17]Powers, 91-98.
[18] Powers, 148.
[19] Lopez, 234.

was without any central influence for the following four – hundred years. In order to fill this vacuum, Tibetan Buddhists gradually expanded as teachers and acolytes moved to galvanise its place in the sangha. Moreover, this expansion fostered the development of monasteries that provided economic wherewithal to its citizens to cement Buddhism as a 'modus vivendi.' The power vacuum resulted in the absence of one dominant sect; the rise of the Mongol Empire around 1234 that led to Sakya Pandita ceding authority to Godan Khan in order to avoid subjugation by the Mongols.[20] The relationship between the two sparked the commencement of a patron-priest relationship between the Mongols and Tibet. The Mongols provided military vigor and protection from outside interests in exchange for spiritual direction, while ceding governance to Tibetans. There are conflicting accounts, notably China, who insist that Tibet was within China's jurisdiction due to the Mongols stagnation of power and collapse that led to the resurgence of China in the region. However, Hugh Richardson interprets "Tibetan submission was to the Mongol khans, and not the emperor of China. When China was annexed to the Mongol empire, it was part of a vast territory that covered much of Asia and later parts of Eastern Europe. After the demise of Mongol power, many regions regained their independence, including both China and Tibet, but no Tibetans participated in China's liberation, nor did any Chinese play any role in Tibet's return to indigenous rule."[21] The Sakya sect ruled Tibet until approximately 1358. During this period, China was ruled by the Yuan

---

[20] Smith Jr,.

[21] Richardson, Hugh. <u>Tibet and Its History.</u> London: Oxford University Press, 1962. P.36.

dynasty until it was toppled by the Ming dynasty. The Ming continued to rule until 1644 during which time they exerted no administrative authority over Tibet.[22]

The Yellow Hat sect or Geluk was originated by an Amdo monk, Tsongkapa, who came to invest Buddhist values that had been in decline, with regards to celibacy and study of the Buddhist doctrine. Geluk, in Tibetan, implies, "the system of virtue." Tsongkapa attracted a devout following that led to the construction of two large monasteries, (Drepung -1416, Sera- 1419) which were located outside of Lhasa that accommodated over fifteen thousand monks by 1950.

The dichotomy of Buddhist lineages became clearer with Tsongkapa's introduction of a stricter moral code that was punctuated by a change in apparel from red to yellow; hence, "Red Hat" To "Yellow Hat" sect.[23] The introduction of the "Yellow Hat" sect created a bitter rivalry with the established "Red Hat" order that supported the Karma Kargyu lineage. In fact, according to Goldstein, the Karma Kargyu where the first to establish the practice of reincarnation in 1193, long before the Yellow Hat sect came into existence. The Dalai Lama is the principle of Tibetan Buddhism and a follower of the Yellow Hat sect that utiilise re-incarnation to select a Dalai Lama, and is a precept in Buddhism.

The Qing dynasty was consolidating power in China at approximately the same period that the Géluka were Tibet's spiritual and temporal leaders. According to Goldstein, the Dalai Lama had the support of Tibetan followers and the Mongolian army, which the Qing revered and led to stability in Tibet until 1705.[24] During this period of power sharing in Tibet, China observed Llabsang Khan as ruler, giving Tibet protection in

_____

[22]Goldstein, Melvyn C. The Snow Lion And The Dragon. London: University of California Press, 1997, p. 4.
[23] Goldstein, 5.
[24] Goldstein, 8 & 12.

exchange for payments. Indeed, the priest-patron relationship had shifted to China from Mongolia, which exasperated the community, in addition to Lhabsang Khan's denouncement of the sixth Dalai Lama, whom he felt was not authentic. The Qing emperor had endorsed the exile of the Dalai Lama to Beijing, with his replacement being of similar characteristics. This set the stage for a major conflict in 1717 between Lhabsang Khan, his loyalists and the Dzungar who were supporting the Géluk and their followers. This conflict began a process of transformation in Tibet's administration with the death of Lhabsang Khan during the battle. In the aftermath, the fraudulent sixth Dalai Lama was removed and replaced with the reincarnate Dalai Lama from Litang; the Qing emperor and his supporter's maintained control over the process, while constraining the power of the aristocracy. An army of Qing loyalists, along with the seventh Dalai Lama moved into Tibet to defeat the Dzungars, and take control of the region. The Qing emperor was interested in Tibet for geopolitical reasons as Goldstein states, not absorbing Tibet into China proper. [25]

The Qing sent five armies into Tibet during the 18th century, most notably to repel a Nepalese invasion and observe the administration practices that they deemed poor and inadequate. A written plan adopted in 1792, proceeded to give traction to reforms: "Twenty-Nine Regulations for Better Government in Tibet." Among the changes was the elevation in status of the ambans of political authority consistent with The Dalai Lama's control over principle administrative affairs and appointments of high-ranking ministers. In the aftermath of the reforms, the ambans maximised their authority, however, they made no effort to assimilate Tibet into China. Goldstein emphasises that Tibet

---

[25] Goldstein, 13 & 14.

"maintained its own language, officials, and legal system, and paid no taxes or tribute to China." Moreover, the adoption of these reforms included the creation of Tibet's first permanent army that would enable Tibet to defend itself, thus, diffusing the need for China to send troops.[26]

The advent of the 19th century in China ushered in a period of weakness as a result of the Opium War (1839-1842) and the Taiping Rebellion (1848-1865). Tibet optimized strength internally as the ambans influence was minimized concurrent to the fall in the influence of the Qing emperors.[27] China's hold over Tibet became nebulous as the thirteenth Dalai Lama was elected in 1877 without utilising the process of the lottery through the "golden urn" that the Qing emperor had instilled in 1792. In addition, in 1895 the Dalai Lama pursued the independent appointments of high-ranking bureaucrats without input from the ambans.[28]

Tibet, due its strategic position, garnered interest from Russia that created uncertainty, which thrust British India into an aggressive approach to protect their trade interests in Tibet. As Smith states, China was vulnerable and unable to make Tibet acquiesce to trade agreements between China and India. Britain seized Lhasa in 1904 that prompted the Dalai Lama to flee Tibet for Urga before visiting China where he was co-opted to power-share with the ambans in Lhasa. China's army moved into Lhasa after the Dalai Lama's return to impose its criteria for the "reorganizing and modernizing" of Tibet to extend its

---

[26] Goldstein, 19-20. Ambans were high-ranking government officials that were representative of the Qing dynastic period. The Qing selection process for The Dalai Lama and Panchen Lama involved a lottery conducted in a golden urn to inhibit "politically powerful lay families" from gerrymandering the incarnation process.
[27] Goldstein, p.21. The Opium War was a conflict between the British East India Company and the Qing Dynasty over China's opposition to free trade, primarily in opium.
[28] Smith Jr, 9.

influence. As a precursor to the 1959 uprising, the Dalai Lama would escape to India in 1910. Goldstein proclaims that the British left Lhasa after the Chinese paid them an indemnity of £562,500, which prompted China to assume a vigilant modus operandi in Tibetan affairs. In addition, China developed interest in Tibetan "cultural, economic, and political integration" in order to protect its interests domestically.[29] However, with an uprising in China, the Chinese army was forced to retreat, which allowed the Dalai Lama to return to Lhasa. Still, with the Dalai Lama extolling independence, the Chinese precipitated their claim to Tibet as a Chinese province. In 1914 a treaty signed by Britain and China divided Tibet into two parts: Central Tibet, from Ladakh to Chamdo that was the Dalai Lama's jurisdiction despite the presence of a small contingent of Chinese officials, and the eastern portion, particularly, Kham, which was controlled by the Chinese administration with the Dalai Lama retaining command over the monasteries. However, China did not validate this treaty and were preoccupied supporting Europe during both World Wars, leaving Tibet to continue its ascription to medieval customs while the world was modernizing around it, preserving a "modus vivendi" with China .[30] In 1945, at the conclusion of WWII, Chiang Kai-shek, Chairman of the National Government of China, in the anti-colonial spirit of the time, promised Tibet and other nationalities self-determination ranging from "a very high degree of autonomy" to independence.[31]

However, by the end of World War Two, China began to regain influence with the ascension of Communism in 1949, and set their target to occupy and control Tibet.

---

[29] Goldstein, 24-26.
[30] Stein, R.A. Tibetan Civilisation. Stanford: Stanford University Press, 1972, p.88-90.
[31] Smith Jr, 11.

China signed a treaty with India that circumvented Indian influence in Tibet while beginning the changes to Tibetan society that included assimilating Tibet into China as a member of the PRC. In retrospect, Tibetans would not have predicted their status as an ethnic minority because China did not hinder their autonomy, and allowed for the preservation of Buddhist tenets, which recognised the freedoms of the Panchen Lama, Dalai Lama and religious structure for Tibetans.[32] Initially, the Chinese assured Tibetans that new roads, hospitals, and schools were central to Chinese efforts to modernity for all Tibetans. Instead, "a movie theatre, bank, and hospital" were constructed with a caveat- they were accessible only to Chinese officials and Tibetan colluders, not the Tibetan populace.[33]

China, in its fledgling post WW2 stage inside Tibet, shifted from a policy of accepting multi-ethnic regions as part of autonomous territories with the right to separate, towards a stance that prohibited these autonomous territories from "breaking away." For Tibet nationalists and followers of the Dalai Lama and Buddhism, this was the start towards Chinese sovereignty in Tibet as one of the principal goals of the newly organized People's Liberation Army, in1949.[34] Tibet, in engaging the international community, was unsure of how to operate in a post WW2 environment in order to protect its history, geography, and religious beliefs, hence, their reticence from enlisting in the United Nations or recruiting outside help until further along into the Chinese occupation. When

---

[32] Stein, p.90.

[33] Powers, p.198. The Chinese felt that Marxism was a panacea for the problems of all societies, however, Tibetans entrenched in Buddhism felt the need to look beyond the banality of secular life. This ran counter to the Chinese who thought Tibetans would unite with them to overthrow the feudalist nature of Tibetan foundations and leadership.

[34] Goldstein, p.41.

Tibet appealed to the UN they were ignored because of the inherent ideological differences that the west faced against communist China (and the Soviet Union) and the possibility of waging a debacle in foreign affairs circles. In addition, with war being waged on the Korean peninsula, the UN, and particularly the U.S. and Soviet Union, were using the Korean conflict to foster a proxy war against each other. Consequently, Tibet's appeal to the UN received short shrift because it was assumed that China would disregard any calls to leave the Tibetan plateau, which would weaken the UN's position in the international community. Thus, Tibet was forced into a position of subservience to the PRC.[35] The Chinese and Tibetan governments agreed to the "Sino – Tibetan Agreement of 1951" that created seventeen stipulations for co-existence. Tibetans believed the strength of the agreement would safeguard their cultural and social independence while guaranteeing that their existing political system would remain and operate as usual, and that the authority and freedoms of the ruling elite would not be constrained. In addition, the agreement promised to protect all their religious freedoms. Oddly, the document made no mention of the terms "communism" or "socialism." Chairman Mao realized the distinctiveness of Tibet initially, when he proclaimed:

> "We must do our best and take the proper steps to win over the Dalai Lama and the majority of his top echelon and to isolate the handful of bad elements in order to achieve a gradual, bloodless transformation of the Tibetan economic and political system over a number of years; on the other hand we must be prepared for the eventuality of the bad elements leading the Tibetan troops in rebellion in attacking us."[36]

---

[35]Shakya, Tershing. <u>The Dragon In The Land of Snows.</u> New York: Columbia University Press, 1999, 52-55.

[36] Tse-tung, Mao. "On The Policies For Our Work In Tibet—Directive Of The Central Committee Of The Communist Party Of China". <u>From The Selected Works Of Mao Tse-tung.</u> Foreign Languages Press. Vol V, 1977, pp. 73-76. July 4, 2009. <http://www.marx2mao.com/Mao/WT52.html>.

 Goldstein notes that Mao Tse-tung preferred cordial relations between Han Chinese and Tibetans in order to soften Tibetan fearfulness, so that Tibet's elite would accept "reintegration" with the Chinese, and agree to the social changes that were being implemented. PLA troops began to label themselves as "New Chinese" in order to present a moderate persona apart from their native brethren. To further establish goodwill, beginning in 1951 through to 1959, property was not confiscated from any aristocrats or monastics; while feudal lords were allowed to maintain their judicial authority over hereditary bound peasants.[37] In its nascent period, with Mao's direction, as mentioned, the Chinese occupiers were accommodating, however, by the mid- 1950s Chinese hardliners were pressing for faster reforms that lead to unrest with refugees from ethnographic Tibet. Mao offered goodwill concessions to the Dalai Lama to continue the "gradualist policy" by reducing the number of troops in combat, the amount of Han cadre, while promising the Dalai Lama in writing that socialist land reforms would be stayed for the next six years. However, Mao made no guarantees to the Dalai Lama that China would not implement those changes regardless of the conditions.

The U.S. was beginning to train and arm Tibetan guerrillas in 1957, however the situation in Tibet was past the point of no return. By early 1959 the Dalai Lama could not control the unrest, and by March a full-scale conflict ensued in Lhasa that forced the Dalai Lama to flee to India when he abandoned the precepts of the "Seventeen Point Agreement." Pent up frustration over deteriorating conditions indicate that Mao's gradualist policy did not succeed. The result for China was the last opportunity to mollify Tibetans to accept the merits of the communist system, which were eroding with each passing day.

---

[37] Goldstein, 52.

Conversely, Tibet's ruling elite failed to create and institute government and social policies to sustain a long-term strategy that would have enabled Tibetans to maximize their long-term autonomy, and encourage the Chinese to acquiesce to their requests.[38] The PRC, buoyed by the exit of the Dalai Lama, began to "fast track" changes to the ruling structure in Tibet. The only vestige of the former power structure of combat lie in the Dalai Lama's position as chairman of the Preparatory Committee, because, ironically, the Chinese felt he was being held in India.

---

[38] Goldstein 55-57. Tibet was ill-prepared to manage any kind of counter-offense both politically or militarily without international support in an expanded role.

Vi Lugs Srol (Sunny Tradition)   Ladakh, India

The Ladakhi population is a caste group that comprises an atypical array of theological, racial (Hindus, Muslims, Sikhs, Tibetans,) musicians and tradespeople, with Tibetan Buddhism as the focal point of faith-based society. Mann elaborates that inhabitants (Ladhakis) denotes a particular ethnic group which includes the euphemisms: Bhot, Bod, Bodh, Bot-pa, and Bhautta (Bota.) The term "Bhot" refers to Buddhists from Tibet.[39] Spanish artist, Leire Ramos Castro who did the cover for this work, had traveled to Ladakh on holiday and provided these still images that illuminate the warmth and culture that Tibetan Buddhism has brought to the area. She explains the problem with altitude sickness that took one week to overcome..."the feeling was like you are far far away" with the evening temperatures dropping to -25 on some occasions and warm during the day. However, she says that the sheer beauty of the "infinite landscapes" and mountains more than compensate for the cooler temperatures. "You are in a totally amazing place, ...and can feel the true essence of Buddhism" where "monks and people live in an ancient Buddhist culture."[40] Mann states that Ladakhis have a cheerful disposition and this can manifest through their singing and dancing, which is considered their favourite form of leisure. Ladakh is recognised as the 'Land of High Passes' and is known for its festivals. With its high altitude it retains its natural splendor; the population base is a contributing factor. The Buddhist sangha is evident in Leire's photographs depicting a 'cradle to grave' monastic lifestyle that is in stark contrast to what is experienced in developed economies or traditional capitalism and socialist systems.

---

[39] Mann, R.S. Ladakh Then And Now. New Delhi: Mittal Publications. 2002.
[40] Leire Castro can be reached at leyreramoscastro@gmail.com. Many thanks to Leire for allowing the use of her photos.

Sems Shugs Chag "Panchen Lama's Petition Sparks Reproach

The Panchen Lama was the only remaining principle voice and was the acting chairman of PCTAR (Preparatory Committee for the Tibet Autonomous Region). In May 1962 the Panchen Lama issued a petition to Zhou Enlai, known as the "70,000 Character Petition" or formally as "A Report on the Sufferings of the Masses in Tibet and Other Tibetan Regions and Suggestions for Future Work to the Central Authorities through the Respected Premier Zhou," indicating the strife that the Chinese reforms were having on the Tibetan people. The Panchen Lama sounded a cautious note that paid tribute to his policies out of respect for the CCP, while attributing the seeds of the revolts to class struggle instead of national conflict. Still, the Panchen Lama was emphatic that Tibet's national identity and Buddhist beliefs were being jeopardized and consequently, allegiance to the Chinese government was questionable. This document is important because it discloses many of the indiscretions of the PRC in Tibet, that were not made public until 1996. The Panchen Lama was a credible source because he was educated in Buddhist and Marxist ideologies. His eight criticisms in the document included:

1) Extreme suppression against people involved in the 1959 uprising.

2) Improper confiscation of property by cadres of those who were under suspicion of being involved in the revolt and subjected to *thamzing*.

3) Harvests were good between 1959-1961 (the years of the Great Leap Forward); however, cadres overstated production levels for self-aggrandizement. The result was the delivery of large amounts of food into China that left the Tibetans with food shortages.

4) Arbitrary attacks against feudal lords and their agents and some well-off surfs were indiscriminately targeted creating fear and mistrust against the PRC.

5) Party cadres did not listen to ordinary citizens who were dictated against and criticized. PCTAR reported that everything was going well in Tibet when, in fact, there were problems in the chain of command that was vague with respect to the Preparatory Committee.

6) Tibetans were arrested en masse after the revolt and had been imprisoned without trial or proof of guilt. Between 10-15% of the population were affected. People died in labor camps and prisons because of poor treatment. Many were executed for opposing the Chinese.

7) Monasteries were labeled as one of the three pillars of feudalism. Those individuals that participated in the uprising should not be discriminated against. Plus, the entire monastic institution and religion were attacked. Cadres eliminated sutras, shrines and Buddhist images. Monks and nuns were forced to secularize.

8) Religion, language, national dress and customs were suppressed in order to assimilate Han Chinese. The Panchen Lama recognised the difficulties to assimilate Han Chinese alongside Tibetans through a distant central authority in Beijing. The quest to appease all parties without outright revolt was problematic; Tibetans did not want to feel they were betraying their principles and motherland, as did the Han Chinese in Tibet. Repercussions for either "dissenters" were becoming more apparent.

Although, the Panchen Lama praised China's efforts, he was reticent to acknowledge his concerns. Despite his tact, the Chinese instituted a propaganda offensive to dishonor him.

In 1964, after refusing to denounce the Dalai Lama, he was removed from his position as head of the PCTAR and received 17 days of thamzing. He was accused of murder, planning to launch a guerrilla war against the state, illicitly cohabitating with women, support for the Dalai Lama, and "criticizing and opposing China in the 70,000 character document." He was transferred to Beijing to live under house arrest and was imprisoned until his release in 1977. The Panchen Lama's removal from his position and exile was clear evidence that the PRC did not feel the need for a Tibetan representative from the old regime, and made it clear that China was in total control. Smith argues correctly that there was no need for these actions because the document was kept secret, however, Mao Tse-tung was apoplectic, which led to the Panchen Lama's expulsion from Tibet.[41]

Bar Gnas: Hu Yaobang

Moderate former Communist Party General Secretary Hu Yaobang, who brought reforms to Tibet after an official visit in 1980, spoke to 5,000 cadres in Lhasa during his visit:

> Our present situation is less than wonderful because the Tibetan people's lives
>
> have not been much improved. There are some improvements in some parts, but
>
> in general, Tibetans still live in relative poverty. In some areas the living
>
> standards had even gone down… we feel that our party has let the Tibetan people

---

[41] Smith Jr., 74-75, 78-94. This is a brief description of the eight points that were contained in the70,000 character text. Thamzing, the Tibetan term for "struggle sessions" pitted the state against individuals, accusing them of false crimes. The object was to remove deterrents against Communism, thus having a cleansing effect.

down… we have worked nearly 30 years, but the life of the Tibetan people has not been notably improved.[42]

The aftermath of Hu's statement led to an opening in Tibet of Han Chinese to enable construction projects that marked a new point in Tibetan history: non-Tibetans were now equal to or surging ahead of ethnic Tibetans in number. According to Goldstein, non-Tibetans were omnipresent in the local economy "from street corner bicycle repairmen to computer storeowners to large firms trading with the rest of China."[43]

Security was strengthened and an economic plan was put in place to bring up GDP and standards for all Tibetans. Projects were initiated that brought more Han Chinese into Tibet to foster development, which is the prevailing theme up to the recent period.[44]

In 1984, negotiations began with the Dalai Lama and Beijing that crystallised in1988 at a convention in Strasbourg, France, that were partly influenced by rioting in Lhasa. The PRC proposed that the Dalai Lama could live in Tibet if he relinquished his desire for independence. At Strasbourg, the Dalai Lama responded that his vision of Tibet was similar to Tibet's position under the Qing dynasty that would have given Tibet autonomy within the PRC. This placed the burden on China to mitigate its position with a compromise. Beijing's response was to reject the offer as they deemed it a step towards

---

[42] Yao, Wang. "Hu Yaobang's Visit To Tibet, May 22–31, 1980. An important Development In The Chinese Government's Tibet Policy." Resistance And Reform In Tibet. Ed. Robert Barnett and Shirin Akiner. Bloomington and Indianapolis: Indiana University Press, 1994. 288.

[43] Goldstein. 94.

[44] Goldstein. 91-94. The Panchen Lama is the second most prominent spiritual leader in Tibet, next to the Dalai Lama. Hu Yuobang's death a week prior had brought the students out to memorialize him and pay tribute to his reform mindedness.

separation. Goldstein rightly states, that China would have difficulty proposing increased freedom for Tibetan's, but not its own citizens within their borders.[45]

The sudden death of the Panchen Lama in 1989 provided an opportunity for the Dalai Lama to strengthen relations with Beijing as Chinese officials were hosting a memorial for the Panchen Lama. The Dalai Lama, concerned about the perceived political fallout (in the eyes of his countrymen) from visiting Beijing (who indicated that he would not be permitted inside Tibet,) declined the offer. Scholars advocate this as the best opportunity to advance Tibetan autonomy since the occupation.[46] 1989 signaled a change with pressure points being placed on Beijing due to the Dalai Lama being awarded the Nobel Peace Prize, and China's deadly response to the student protesters in Tiananmen Square. Beijing adopted a new policy that left the Dalai Lama 'outside the circle' as a means to resolve the Tibet problem. Instead, their approach was fortified and contrary to that of proposals formed at Strasbourg.

Ngo Rgol Sger Langs "March 2008 Uprising"

"When (they) the Tibetan monks were shot at… and when they were suppressed violently and beaten, then the Tibetan community exploded, because they are a tinder box, because China has been smothering them…"explains Robert Thurman.[47] The protests grew in scope and the police and undercover agents were keen to force foreigners to erase any

---

[45] Goldstein,84-85.
[46] Goldstein, 87-90.
[47] Roberts John B and Elizabeth Roberts. Freeing Tibet. New York: AMACOM. 2009. 217. Thurman was interviewed on March 20, 2008 by Democracy Now, a radio station.

photos and stay within their accommodations. In fact, the police kept a vigil in front of hotels until transportation arrived to escort tourists out of Tibet. The news blackout was cited as necessary because of the incarceration of tourists.[48] And so another melodramatic moment in Tibet's recent history ensued. In typical fashion each side blamed the other party without offering any compromise or solution. Desperate to portray a benevolent China to the world, Chinese officials orchestrated a trip into Lhasa by foreign journalists to conduct staged interviews at the Jokhang temple. Civilians dressed as monks answered questions, shouted protest slogans, and some openly wept. However, a few were quite honest with reporters who filed their story before Chinese officials could move them from the area. To bring the story of the unrest and plight of the Tibetans into the public sphere, then U.S. House Speaker Nancy Pelosi appealed to proponents of human rights to speak out, that resulted in a protest movement from Paris, to the U.S. and to Katmandu.[49] Reports of casualties during the two-month period of unrest were 22 Han Chinese killed as disclosed by the Chinese authorities, while the TGIE indicated that 203 Tibetans were killed in Lhasa by Chinese forces. As the Chinese government went into 'damage control' with the Olympics starting in August, they restricted the number of people coming into Tibet, while limiting news content that would reach the rest of the world. In addition, all tourism was halted.

The continued assimilation into Tibet by Han Chinese has brought more wealth into the region from the central government. However, the Han typically receive priority in public sector positions. As the Han have gained more prominence, they look down on native Tibetans for their effusive attachment to religion. Professor Barry Sautman illustrates this

---

[48] Roberts John B and Elizabeth Roberts 217.
[49] Roberts John B and Elizabeth Roberts 219-220.

point: "Many Han migrants have racist attitudes toward Tibetans, mostly notions that Tibetans are lazy, dirty, and obsessed with religion. Many Tibetans reciprocate with representations of Han as rich, money obsessed and conspiring to exploit Tibetans."[50] These are some of the reasons that resulted in the Lhasa protest, that, in conjunction with the onset of the Olympics, brought global attention to circumstances in Tibet. Sautman, a proponent of Beijing's stance, condemns the separatists who "know they can count on the automatic sympathy of Western politicians and media, who view China as a strategic economic and political competitor" and "who would never allow riots like these to go unchallenged in their country." Sautman is correct in this regard when he draws comparisons to the riots in Los Angeles in 1992, in which then President George H W Bush stated that he would use whatever force is necessary to quell the demonstrations."[51] Professor Sautman is absolutely correct in displaying the double standard towards China in international relations. However, contrary to Sautman's claims, the Dalai Lama did indicate on March 18, 2008 that he would step down if violence continues in Tibet. Moreover, the continued oppression and occupation of Tibet and Tibetans has now been going on for over fifty years; not an isolated incident."[52] With pressure on China during the protest, then President Hu Jintao relented on April 26, 2008, inviting the Dalai Lama to send delegates to Beijing to address the situation in Tibet. The Chinese response was

---

[50] Sautman Barry. "Protests in Tibet and Separatism: the Olympics and Beyond." Permanent Mission of the People's Republic of China to the UN. 16 April 2008. 3 August 2009 < http://www.mfa.gov.cn/ce/ceun/eng/gyzg/xizang/t425983.htm>.
[51] Sautman, Barry.
<http://www.mfa.gov.cn/ce/ceun/eng/gyzg/xizang/t425983.htm>.

[52] CBC News. France Ponders Boycott OF Beijing Over Tibet Conflict. CBCNEWS.ca. 18 March 2008. 4 August 2009
<http://www.cbc.ca/world/story/2008/03/18/china-tibet.html>.

that they were only interested in the Dalai Lama's help to improve the situation in Tibet. They rejected the idea of an autonomous Tibetan state encompassing ¼ of China; they disagreed on a demilitarized area as a precursor to independence, and admonished the Dalai Lama for his international involvement, which are primarily religious in scope. Preceding the opening of the Olympic games, the Dalai Lama modified his "Middle Way" approach to the Chinese by conceding that an autonomous Tibet would maintain its position as part of China. Hu Jintao was urged to invite the Dalai Lama to Beijing in November 2008. Unfortunately, there was no offer from the Chinese President. Many believe that this inaction supports the notion that the PRC is waiting for the Dalai Lama to die, and with that, any hope for increased autonomy.[53]

Recently, until the Tibetan uprising in March of 2008, the tone between the two sides was somber. Tibetans commemorate the anniversary of the failed uprising on March 10 each year, however, 2008 proved to be a case of fomenting pent up anger among Tibetans, as Chinese propaganda was intent on displaying to the world a sense of calm and achievement in Tibet since the occupation. The Chinese government took a strident approach with rioters, though qualified their response with a stinging rebuke of the Dalai Lama: "This riot was deliberately manipulated by the Dalai Lama clique, and our government has taken legal actions to return Lhasa and other places to normality" the spokesman for the Chinese Foreign Ministry, Qin Gang said. In addition, "The Dalai Lama is not purely a religious person. For a long time, he wore a religious coat and held the balance of peace while trying to separate China and destroy social stability and

---

[53] Roberts John B and Elizabeth Roberts, 225-226.

national unity."[54] The response was unexpected as the Dalai Lama stated that if the violence continues, he would resign as the head of the TGIE. Replying to comments that he is a separatist, he stated: "The Chinese constitution already mentions autonomy for Tibet. So that should not be just a word on paper but implemented on the spot." He continued "The whole world knows Dalai Lama is not seeking independence, one hundred times, a thousand times I have repeated this. It is my mantra – we are not seeking independence."[55]

In 1987, the Dalai Lama proposed a "Five Point Peace Plan" to the United States Congress. In sum, he proposed a peace zone for all of Tibet including Kham and Amdo provinces. Secondly, the end of the population transfers of Han Chinese. Third, restoration of cultural, spiritual, economic, and basic democratic freedoms. Fourth, restoration of the natural environment; no area should be used for the production or dumping of nuclear material or waste. Fifth, negotiations on the relationship between Tibetan and Chinese people respecting the differences that exist between them.[56] China's response to this proposal was that the Dalai Lama was still seeking independence for Tibet. The advent of the civil unrest in China in 1989 coupled with the Dalai Lama's receipt of the Nobel peace prize resulted in muted talks between China and the TGIE. Winning the Nobel peace prize thrust the Dalai Lama into the public stratosphere and

---

[54] Barboza David. "660 Held in Tibetan Uprising, China Says." NYTimes.com. 27 March 2008. 2 August 2009 <http://www.nytimes.com/2008/03/27/world/asia/27tibet.html>.
[55] Buncombe Andrew. "Dalai Lama: I am prepared to face China. I will go to Beijing." Independent.co.uk.com . 21 March 2008. 2 August 2009 <http://www.independent.co.uk/news/world/asia/dalai-lama-i-am-prepared-to-face-china-i-will-go-to-beijing-798998.html>.
[56] His Holiness the Dalai Lama. "Five Point Peace Plan for Tibet." http://www.dalailama.com/messages/tibet/five-point-peace-plan. 22 April 2014 <http://www.tibet.com/proposal/5point.html>.

made him popular among celebrities and dignitaries. Chinese representatives were unhappy with the Dalai Lama bringing the issue of Tibet into the public sphere to gain attention. This impacted the negotiation process at that point in time and continues to the present day when discussions or visits between Western leaders and the Dalai Lama take place.

In March 2008 the situation in Tibet, and Lhasa, in particular, grew tense. The Summer Olympics of 2008 provided an opportunity for the PRC to demonstrate the success of reforms in China, and changes inside Tibet.

Tibetans have lived under threat of reprisal for many years. Simple acts that we take for granted are punishable, such as speaking about a free Tibet or mentioning the Dalai Lama's name. Talking to tourists about politics can result in imprisonment for divulging 'state secrets.' Expressing your views among personal acquaintances' regarding Chinese authoritarianism is punishable. Moreover, as is typical of communist regimes, freedom of speech, religion, assembly and the press do not exist in Tibet.

The 'one-child policy' in effect, Tibetan women have been known to undergo forced abortions if they cannot pay the fine for exceeding the limit. During the procedure, often no anesthesia or pain medication is supplied. After surgery, no after-care is provided.[57]

The correlation between the Dalai Lama's public appearances and unrest in Tibet exists to the present time with displays of unrest by Tibetans followed by Chinese retrenchment. The PRC claim duplicity in that the Dalai Lama and the Tibetan Youth Congress have been linked to the majority of protests in Tibet, using the Dalai Lama's public events to illuminate both their positions as a global voice for reforms in Tibet. Indeed, the outbreak

---

[57] Roberts John B and Elizabeth Roberts 216.

of violence after the Dalai Lama spoke to the U.S. Congress in 1987 evoked condemnation from the Chinese authorities and led to then Governor of Tibet, Hu Jintao to take a hardline approach in 1988 by imposing Martial Law. No specific proof could be attributed to the TYC; however, the act prompted the Chinese to commence an enormous media drive in Tibet to slam the U.S. involvement in China's domestic matters and accusing the Dalai Lama of trying to fracture the nation. The strong reply to the speech in Congress led Tibetans to have confidence that the American government had a genuine interest in the Tibet issue.[58]

Democratisation and Discrimination: A Paradox for China

Dbye byed: Discrimination

"Discrimination requires three persons at a minimum: (1) the Discriminator, (2) The Discriminatee, the person discriminated against, and (3) the parties who have been favoured in comparison with the discriminates."[59]

The issue of racism in Tibet follows this simple description by Professor Narveson to illustrate the Tibet situation. It might be worthwhile to employ Narveson's notion of "inadvertent discrimination" when we speak of the Tibet Problem. Surely, the PRC does not keep a list of every single Tibetan and thus, targets them unilaterally. As evidence from various uprisings have shown, Chinese police respond *cohibeo* to those individuals they view as perpetrators. However, now that we are at a point in Tibet where the influx

---

58 Shakya, 416-417.

59 Narveson, Jan. "Have We A Right To Non-Discrimination?" Business Ethics In Canada. Ed. _Poff, Deborah C. and Wilfred J. Waluchow. Scarborough: Prentice-Hall, 1991. 279.

of Han Chinese has placed ethnic Tibetan's at a disadvantage, the question remains: Is

racism a problem between Tibetans and Han Chinese in the political sphere, and if it is,

what is the solution? Also, is the voice of Tibetan human rights groups being constrained

in the international community?

Historically, Tibetans being of a nomadic nature, lived in the mountains during the

summer and moved back to their ancestral grounds and lower altitude during the winter

where it is warmer. As Chinese settlers moved into these "ancestral lands" they viewed

Tibetans as barbaric and unorthodox. During the summer period, Tibetans retreat to their

mountain region while Chinese settlers moved into their ancestral lands. As Tibetans

moved back into their region during the winter period and reclaimed their land, conflict

ensued.[60] The incursion of Han Chinese began as a moderate process, however, after the

occupation, the PRC has increased the numbers significantly. The root of the problem lies

with China's intent to modernise Tibet. Proponents of environmental reform advocate

maintaining conditions in regions that have a delicate system and require human

interference to offset the drive for resource procurement, in order to maximize profits,

and in Tibet's case, "modernisation. " Goldstein explains that the huge incursion of

Chinese and Muslims since 1984 is not a deliberate attempt to reshape Tibetan culture,

instead, it is the need to acquire skilled labour to manage projects in order to improve

Tibet's infrastructure. The pejorative effect on ethnic Tibetans was the expansion of

Chinese goods and services to accommodate the Han migrants. Moreover, the rise in

---

[60] International Campaign For Tibet. Jampa: The Story Of Racism In Tibet.September
2001. 16 August 2009. USA: ICT, 26. < http://www.savetibet.org/wp-
content/uploads/2013/01/JampaRacism.pdf >. This document was prepared for
the United Nations World Conference Against Racism that took place September
2001 in Durban, South Africa. Tibetan NGO's were shut out of the accreditation
process by the Chinese who viewed their presence as splittist.

migrants and labour sent signals to surrounding regions and Han that work is plentiful in Tibet, which continues to the present. Tibetans wanted economic reforms but not at the expense of their culture and jobs. Indeed, they feel ostracised due to the power structure shifting away from them; cultural and religious impediments, and bitterness about the occupation. Religious barriers that were put in place by Beijing to limit the number of monks in monasteries, created dissension and has fostered anti- Sino sentiment, exactly the opposite effect that Beijing had in mind to reduce nationalist fervor in Lhasa.[61] To further encourage feelings of partisanship, Tibetans seeking employment in the state sector are basically shut out of the system. Up to 2003, Han Chinese represented approximately 6% of the TAR, (see their employment levels in the cadres - those permanently employed in government jobs) expand, while ethnic Tibetans saw their share drop from over 70% to less than 50% in only five years. To compound matters, exams are given in Mandarin for applicants seeking public sector jobs. Education at the university level is almost exclusively taught in Mandarin and is taking on more prominence in all higher levels of education.[62] The notion of racism, while appearing accidental has reached fruition and will continue to lead to domination by Han Chinese in labour and trade sectors.

---

[61] Goldstein. 84-85. Goldstein illuminates the issue by stating that Tibet was the exclusive home to Tibetans, and that no Han Chinese had emigrated there by 1950; this has disillusioned older Tibetans who have seen their way of life change dramatically.

[62] refworld "World Directory of Minorities and Indigenous Peoples-China: Tibetans."July 2008. 21 April 2014.
< http://www.refworld.org/docid/49749d3dc.html http://www.unhcr.org/cgi-bin/texis/vtx/refworld/rwmain?page=printdoc&docid=49749d3dc>.

"Migrant Han entrepreneurs elbow out Tibetan rivals, then return home for the winter after reaping profits. Large Han-owned companies dominate the main industries, from mining to construction to tourism."[63]

China's Prospects for Democratisation

The goal of Tibetan statehood most likely draws on the collapse of the PRC, similar to the failure of the Former Soviet Union. However, as the PRC has a template to draw on regarding Mikhail Gorbachev's failed policies of 'Perestroika' to restructure the economy, and 'Glasnost' to procure more openness in the political system, China has focused on developing the economy, particularly in the aftermath of the Tiananmen Square crisis. These decisions have resulted in major economic growth that continues to the present and is helping to fund and revitalise their military and colonial ambitions. This is being accomplished through the expansion of the private sector, FDI (Foreign Direct Investment,) the surge in Chinese exports, and decline of SOE's (State-Owned Enterprises.) However, China's piecemeal approach to opening the political system has been limited primarily to the cadres and villages in rural areas, where multi – party elections are well contained. Still, corruption is very problematic for China's ruling elites to manage and is a tinderbox for citizen revolt due to land grabs and inadequate protection for workers from overzealous employers (who perish without paying wages

---

[63] Wong, Edward. "China's Money and Migrants Pour Into Tibet." <u>New York Times</u>. 24 July 2010. 23 April 2014.
<http://www.nytimes.com/2010/07/25/world/asia/25tibet.html?pagewanted=all &_r=0>.

that are owed,) and poor working conditions that include the demands of 16 hour work-shifts. Owing to the dissension is the absence of unions to support workers claims against these employers. Strikes are the main recourse for workers to draw attention to their plight, what we regard in North America as 'wildcat strikes,' although some workers remain at the job-site and simply put their tools down or stop working. Regarding property rights, Chinese officials, in some cases have simply sold public land without reimbursing those being affected. To their credit, Chinese officials are reacting to these protests before they become visible in the press or social media circles. China's lack of checks and balances at the cadre and/or village level creates worry for the PRC, that has historically operated with an internal 'locus of control' regarding most state matters. Minxin Pei notes that..."historically, no communist regime has ever completed an evolutionary process of the Democratic transition. He explains that there is little appetite to cede power as affluence becomes the quid pro quo for sustained influence and control over the masses and the political system. Economic growth has sustained the PRC and offered promise to many Chinese who migrate to urban centers for employment opportunities. Thus, Pei states that rising prosperity reduces the pressure to reform and provides the stimulus to maintain the oppressive conduit and corruption. [64] Are democratisation and discrimination different? Democratisation offers more rights for upper strata income groups regardless of political sphere. A well-developed state such as the PRC already holds the necessary social constructs to diminish the effects of a change in political philosophy. There are risks in that guise which resulted in civil chaos in Iraq after Saddam Hussein was deposed, for example. The International Community may be

---

[64] Pei, Minxin. China's Trapped Transition: The Limits of Developmental Autocracy. Cambridge: Harvard University Press, 2006.

provided with an opportunity to help Tibetans in the aftermath of a collapse. The notion of 'positive' and 'negative' rights should be considered when engaging the Tibet question. Is there a moral obligation to act in Tibet's defense by the International Community now, or in the future should democracy rise and bring with it many new challenges. Left unchecked, we see the errors of our ways through the lens of Rwanda and Darfur. The United Nations "Human Development Report 2013" indicates that Tibet is last, within China, at .63% on the HDI index. [65] Because of the growing number of protest movements, China's wealth is asymmetrical. Income is dispersed mainly to the most affluent citizens, and government officials, (Forbes indicates that "the total income of the top 20 percent of rural households was 10.19 times higher than the bottom 20 percent," while more focus needs to be put on rural economic development to assuage those feeling left out and more inclined towards unrest.[66] Democratisation appears to continue along a slow path, inhibiting Tibet's chances for easing of Beijing's strict policies. Despite the political system, racism is present in developed countries and is continuing to evolve as population growth becomes more diversified.

---

[65] United Nations Development Programme. Human Development Report 2013. Director and Lead Author, Khalid Malik. 2013. April 15 2014. <http://hdr.undp.org/sites/default/files/reports/14/hdr2013_en_complete.pdf>. GINI coefficient data, indicating income inequality, shows China's overall index falling to .474 in 2012 from a high of .491 in 2008 when the global financial crisis struck. A value of 0 gauges total equality; a value of 100= total inequality.
[66] Rapoza, Kenneth. "The China Miracle: A Rising Wealth Gap." Forbes January 20, 2013. April 20, 2014. < http://www.forbes.com/sites/kenrapoza/2013/01/20/the-china-miracle-a-rising-wealth-gap/>.

Looking back at the photos from Ladakh, the sense of sangha or community among Buddhists presents the panacea for what ails social systems in our world. When China democratises there will still be racism, or do we call it something else because it is less harmful.

Discrimination

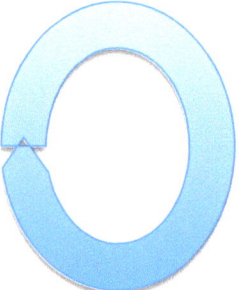

Democratisation

The reality is, is that discrimination and democratisation are at work simultaneously within each system. Consider the notions of social welfare and means testing, taxation, distribution of income, and religious freedoms that affect each of us, particularly in the West. The solution is untenable; there is only one Ladakh, though Ladakh is there for everyone to learn from. When we talk of discrimination and the need to democratise in China including Tibet, the onus is on Chinese authorities to recognise their racist policies towards Tibetan women who exceed the one-child policy. Harassment from state officials to undergo forced abortions and severe economic sanctions that the entire family must bear, continue despite China being a signatory of the UN 'Convention on the Elimination of All Forms of Discrimination Against Women, the Convention on the Prevention and Punishment of the Crime of Genocide, and the Convention Against Torture and Other

Cruel , Inhuman or Degrading Treatment or Punishment.[67] Traditionally, Tibetan women have been noted for their strength and ability to socialise and integrate with men at all levels. Sir Charles Bell stated during Tibetan independence prior to the occuparion: "When a traveller enters Tibet from neighbouring China or India, few things impress him vigorously or more deeply than the position of the Tibet women. They are not kept in seclusion, as are Indian women. Accustomed to mix with the other sex throughout their lives, they are at ease with men, and can hold their own as any women in the world.[68] This validates the change in philosophy within Tibet that has occurred under China's rubric of policies that denigrate females, but also contribute to the demise and destruction of the monastic community and Tibetan culture. The consequences of which are being felt through the expression of self-immolations among both genders to garner attention to oppressive living conditions that are harmful and serve only the interests of Chinese officials as a training ground for cultural assimilation, and economic expansion.

Discrimination is endemic in all stratospheres; we can only safeguard against it by appealing to common virtues and kindness, regardless of any preconceived notions about individuals or groups that we have built up over time. Ladhakis are part of a unique caste system that is discriminatory against Muslims and exogenous factors that include Tibetan émigrés who bring with them a lower economic status. Still, in its historical period and current state, it provides a glimpse into how Tibetan Buddhism was once practiced within

---

[67] Eva Herzer and Sara B. Levin. "China's Denial Of Tibetan Women's Right To Reproductive Freedom." October 10, 1995. April 20, 2014. <http://www.tibetjustice.org/reports/women/chinas_denial.html>.
[68] Thonsur, Tsering Norzom. "Women: Emancipation in Exile." Exile As Challenge The Tibetan Diaspora. New Delhi: Orient Longman, 2004. 323.

Tibet and not the dystopian model that currently exists. China will face mounting pressure to democratise in the future. For China, democratisation and discrimination are incompatible because of the high economic cost to change, and the maintenance and expansion of social programs. Coupled with the loss in power to ruling elites, democratisation leaves an opportunity for restive provinces such as Tibet, Uyghur, and Xinjiang, that have separatist ambitions, to pursue statehood. The PRC cannot afford the consequences of another mass protest that was experienced in the lead up to, and aftermath of Tiananmen Square (1989.) However, if the International Community provides financial and human resource capital in the advent of the restructuring of the political system, change towards a democratic egalitarian society remains a distinct possibility.

Gnas Stangs Mtho Po (high status): Tibet On The Red Carpet

The West has seen a romantic appeal and connection to Tibetans through the spread of Buddhism as a religion and spiritual way of life. China, by its occupation of Tibet, has given Tibetans and followers in the west, an issue that gives traction and hope to an otherwise dismal situation. American actors such as Brad Pitt introduced moviegoers to Tibet and the Dalai Lama in the film: "Seven Years in Tibet." Richard Gere, a well-known American actor and practicing Buddhist has also brought attention to the Tibetan cause as he has visited the Dalai Lama in Dharamsala and is a vocal supporter and ally. Moreover, fundraising took on a new platform with a series of concerts from 1996-2001, the Tibetan Freedom Concerts that raised 1.2 million. The emergence of Tibet into

Hollywood and a new interest in Tibet and Buddhism, has found a new audience that is influential from a monetary standpoint.[69] Richard Gere assumed leadership of the chairmanship of the International Campaign for Tibet in 1995. In addition he gave a speech to the United Nations Human Rights Commission, the European Parliament, and U.S. Congress. However, Chinese officials were not impressed; in1996 the Chinese authorities made possession of a photograph of the Dalai Lama a criminal offense with a sentence up to seven years in jail.[70] Coincidentally, in 1998, the CIA disclosed for the first time that the U.S. government had been giving 1.7 million per year to the TGIE and resistance, until it became public, which led to then Secretary of State Henry Kissinger cancelling the program. To be sure, the awareness of the Tibet problem can be taken in stride as a benevolent force without presenting any threat to China, as donations are to support the TGIE. Awareness, if channeled consistently can pressure western-based governments to link trade related issues with human rights.

The international community has accepted that China has sovereignty over Tibet despite their view of China as an external actor. Richard Bush III of the Brookings Institute illustrates this fact: "I think to an extent the game is over because the main reason is that no country besides China denies that Tibet is part of China. The U.S. government has said that Tibet is part of China as we recognise the PRC as the sole legal government. It is different from Taiwan where we don't say that. Strictly speaking, we do not associate ourselves with the idea that the territory of Taiwan is a part of the state called China."[71]

---

[69] Roberts John B and Elizabeth Roberts, 196.
[70] Roberts, John B and Elizabeth Roberts,194.
[71] Bush III Richard. "Interview on Tibet." Post-Colonial Transformations in China's Hong Kong & Macao: Implications for Cross-Taiwan Strait and Canada-PRC Links Conference. University of Waterloo, Waterloo. 27 June 2009.

In concert with the international community, the Dalai Lama has muted his claims for independence for Tibet and ascribes to a "Middle Way" approach that envisions China managing defence, foreign affairs, and technical expertise aided through Chinese engineers. Tibetans should manage the economy and spiritual matters. In sum, the Dalai Lama states that..."in those areas that Tibetans can manage, can work, all authority should be in Tibetan hands, but in those fields, where we cannot manage, Chinese experts must come and help." He concludes that where conditions do not suit Tibetans, then Tibetans should be in their control to repudiate those directives from Chinese authorities.[72] It is a proposal that merits rapprochement.

Med Pa Bzo Yag: Solutions

Egalitarian	Autarchic
Outside parties to assist talks	UN/NATO involvement with unrest
Power-sharing agreement	Link environment to trade
UN "buffer zone"	Link human rights to trade
Embassies	Cap FDI to promote democratisation

The PRC and the Dalai Lama have been in negotiations for approximately 25 years. Publicly, China views the Dalai Lama with contempt for the Chinese state and have no misgivings about their distrust of him and the 'Dalai Clique' that consist of expatriates

---

[72] Dagmar Bernstorff and Hubertus Von Welck. "An Interview with Tenzin Gyatso, the Fourteenth Dalai Lama." Exile As Challenge The Tibetan Diaspora. New Delhi: Orient Longman, 2004. 113-114.
[73] The World Bank. "GDP Ranking." 2012. 7 March 2014.
<http://databank.worldbank.org/data/download/GDP.pdf >.

living in Dharamsala, as nationalists inside Tibet, or as part of the Diaspora. As a result

of the PRC's dramatic crackdowns on Tibetan protesters, particularly in the lead-up to

Beijing's Olympic games in 2008, and subsequent recriminations against the PRC by the

Dalai Lama, negotiations have taken a protracted and acrimonious chart to this point.

The PRC has grown stronger economically since the occupation and Deng Xiaoping's

economic reforms, that have placed China second globally in GDP as of 2012, surpassing

Japan, according to World Bank data. [73] In addition, FDI (Foreign Direct Investment)

has helped drive the Chinese economic miracle to a 2.13 trillion in holdings up to June

2009. The international community has been ambivalent with established economies

fearful of China's desire for political and economic power, leaving them to close

loopholes and raise borders to FDI, while developing economies have opened their doors

to Chinese investment. In cases such as Algeria and Congo, Chinese firms import many

of their own workers, leaving native Algerians in a struggle for jobs, mirroring the

Tibetan situation. In Sudan, Chinese are accused of corroborating with Khartoum during

the conflict in Darfur. Al-Tahir al-Feki, a spokesman for Sudan's rebel Justice and

Equality Movement, noted that the Chinese are only interested in the economic benefits,

and once those rewards are exhausted they will withdraw and leave "many things

destroyed behind them."[74]Any possibility of the TGIE succeeding in gaining

independence has vanquished with the strength of economic reforms in China and their

superb monetary performance. Indeed, with China's robust trade surplus, there is little

---

[73] The World Bank. "GDP Ranking." 2012. 7 March 2014.
<http://databank.worldbank.org/data/download/GDP.pdf >.
[74] Lowe, Christian. "Expansive China faces grass roots resentment." Reuters 18
August 2009. 18 August 2009
<http://www.reuters.com/article/ousiv/idUSTRE57H00220090818>.

sway the international community can muster to pressure the PRC politically. The EU

and US combined for 686 billion dollars in export business from China in 2011[75] while

China has invested approximately130 billion in US bonds or 2/3 of their foreign reserves,

that gives them tacit influence in US foreign affairs and domestic fiscal policy.[76] The

Obama Administration, wary of the duress caused by the prolonged conflicts in

Afghanistan and Iraq, has fuelled a new period in 'Pax Americana' in Sino-U.S. relations

and multilateralism between global super-powers. To demonstrate China's clout

internationally, during then U.S. Secretary of State Hillary Clinton's visit to Beijing in

2009, she made no mention of China's record on human rights, instead, focusing on the

global economic crisis, despite 2009 being the twentieth anniversary of the Tiananmen

Square massacre and Beijing's lamentable record regarding human rights.[77] China's

economic strength has expanded significantly, their military budget from 14.6 billion in

2000 to a 132 billion (U.S.) budget for 2014.[78] This reflects President Xi Jinping's desire

to demonstrate China's goal of protecting its interests in the region, much to the chagrin

---

[75] Starmass.com. 2012. 21 April 2014. < http://www.starmass.com/china-review/imports-exports/china-top-export-market.htm>.

[76] Bradsher Keith. "China Slows Purchases of U.S. and Other Bonds." NYTimes.com. 12 April 2009. 1 August 2009
http://www.nytimes.com/2009/04/13/business/global/13yuan.html?_r=0 >.

[77] Raddatz Martha and Jenna Mucha. "Clinton Seeks To Reassure China On T-Bills." ABC News.go.com. 21 February 2009. 1 August 2009.
<http://abcnews.go.com/International/story?id=6930021&page=1>.

[78] Prathibha, MS. "China's 2014 Defence Budget: An Assessment." IDSA. 21 April 2014. 21 April
2014.<http://www.idsa.in/idsacomments/Chinas2014DefenceBudget_msprathibha_210414>.Xi Jinping prefers to invest in higher technology weaponry, training and equipment   through local resources. The focus is to intensify the upgradation of backward equipment, improve living, training and working conditions for military personnel, according to Sun Huangtian, Vice-Minister of General Logistics Dept. The purpose supports a move to modernise, satisfy and attract qualified military personnel in state supported goals of quelling protests, maintaining order in Tibet, Uyghur, Xinjiang and other flashpoints that have separatist ideals.

of Japan's leadership. [79] Rebuilding the military is crucial since the decay from its Soviet era machinery. The cooling of the Sino-Russia relationship began with skirmishes along the Ussuri River in 1969 when 50 Soviet soldiers were killed by Chinese troops.[80] The principle issue was the disagreement about ownership regarding parcels of land along the Ussuri. Negotiations between Moscow and China had been dragging on for many years. Japan, Taiwan and Russia need to be wary of the large sums China is investing in their military, though, the rejuvenation of its armed forces remains a long-term project. This should not dissuade states in the region from linking issues to human rights, however sensitive the Chinese are regarding 'separatist' states, and their willingness to criticize governments or threaten restrictions on communication. Heads of State in the developed world are often censured for meeting with the Dalai Lama. A recent visit on February 21, 2014 by His Holiness to meet with U.S. President Obama demonstrated Chinese officials reactionary nature as the Chinese Ministry of Foreign Affairs claimed the meeting would "sabotage" and "undermine" relations between the two economic juggernauts.[81]. Regular meetings between the two have been moved from the Oval Office to the Map Room (for the third time during President Obama's tenure) to acquiesce to Beijing's sensitivity to the Tibet issue. The preceding issue with Russia and China indicates the protracted

---

[79] Martina Michael and Greg Torode. "China's Xi ramps up military spending in face of worried region." www.reuters.com. 5 March 2014. 7 March 2014.
< www.reuters.com/article/2014/03/05/us-china-parliament-defence-idUSBREA2403L20140305.>
[80] Burr, William. "The Sino-Soviet Border Conflict, 1969: U.S. Reactions and Diplomatic Maneuvers." 12 June 2001. 21 April 2014.
<http://www2.gwu.edu/~nsarchiv/NSAEBB/NSAEBB49/index2.html>.
[81] Brown, Kerry. "Obama, Xi, and the Dalai Lama: How to Address the Tibet Issue." www.thediplomat.com. 04 March 2014. 08 March 2014.
<http://www.thediplomat.com/2014/03/obama-xi-and-the-dalai-lama-how-to-address-the-tibet-issue/>.

negotiations that can be part and parcel of dealing with the PRC. Indeed, those negotiations had been ongoing for forty years. Whether the TGIE can expect any similar pattern of compromise remains dubious because of the major disadvantage that the TGIE has within Tibet and the International Community. An important aspect of the land agreement between Russia and China is the improvement in political and economic relations between the two countries. The main issues regarding the border markings were resolved in 2004 when President Putin visited China, whereby the PRC approved of Russia's entrance into the WTO (World Trade Organisation).[82] This issue illustrates the need for linkages that will be necessary to urge China to negotiate seriously on Tibet in a power-sharing arrangement or 'Middle Way,' as suggested by the Dalai Lama.

The above chart indicates two approaches to move toward a solution(s) for Tibet and China. An *egalitarian* approach is symbolic of the benefits that diplomacy can bring to the international community. This approach may gain traction, similar to the 'Six Plus Talks' and 'Sunshine Policy' that, while now stagnant regarding North Korea, have brought calm to the Korean Peninsula during negotiations. In the same manner, outside parties enlisted to assist in talks with representatives of the TGIE and Beijing in a short forum, can provide improvement to the situation on the ground in Tibet, where, according to 'International Campaign for Tibet' 127 Tibetans have self-immolated since February 27, 2009 to protest Chinese oppression.[83] For the process to begin, it will be necessary to acquire the influence of former or current heads of state such as Former U.S. President

---

[82] The Economic Times. "China, Russia settle border dispute." 15 October 2004. 21 April 2014. < http://articles.economictimes.indiatimes.com/2004-10-15/news/27395578_1_russia-and-china-diplomatic-ties-tarabarov>.
[83] International Campaign for Tibet. "Self-Immolations by Tibetans." 17 February 2014. 13 March 2014. < http://www.savetibet.org/resources/fact-sheets/self-immolations-by-tibetans/>.

Bill Clinton, Former UK Prime Minister Tony Blair or Canadian Prime Minister Stephen

Harper. The past success of Bill Clinton in North Korea to secure the release of two

hostages gives credibility to this approach as well as Former Canadian Prime Minister

Brian Mulroney's role in repealing Apartheid in South Africa. In a contrasting, *autarkic*

manner, incurring help from the UN or NATO when the next crisis occurs may be a more

radical and interrogate approach towards Beijing. Sanctions may be viewed as a

stratagem to garner China's leadership attention. However, the reality is that Beijing

simply needs to vote against any UN led sanctions to veto the process, leaving sanctions

as a unilateral option for nation-states to express their disapproval of human rights

concerns. However, they risk alienating the PRC, which may harm future political and

economic relations. Thus, the "endgame" that China and Russia enjoy as members of an

exclusive club within the UN, illustrates clearly that the current U.N. Security Council

membership is antiquated and needs to reflect the strength of other burgeoning and

historical powers, such as Japan, Germany, and Brazil. The expansion of the Security

Council will dilute the omnipotence that the current P5 have enjoyed for over 60 years. A

contentious issue like Tibet, put to a vote in an expanded Security Council could reap

more support from countries that are aware of the need to expose and ameliorate human

and environmental rights as global issues, and the need for a balance of power among UN

members. It is important for successful relations between China and the TGIE, as Robert

Thurman explains, that China needs to govern in an altruistic fashion, with a more

spiritual approach that respects their own land and history without falling prey to the

"military-industrial imperialist lifestyle" in their goal to be a global superpower.[84] While

---

[84] Thurman, Robert. <u>Why The Dalai Lama Matters</u>. New York: Beyond Words

it is a global dilemma that has created problems of pollution, ultra competitiveness, and materialism, China can find a new role as a leader economically, environmentally, and spiritually by operating in a comprehensive, humanitarian manner utilizing "soft power" through coopting and not coercion.

China is very concerned about retaining order in Tibet under the rubric of communism. Many affected people, tourists (when they are allowed into Tibet) and citizens that may experience untoward acts of violence from Chinese authorities, have no real legitimate outlet for sanctuary or access to institutions to seek help or advice. Currently, in Tibet there is a single embassy for Nepal in Lhasa.[85] There are some NGO's on the ground such as UNICEF, however, there is nothing that is robust and that can withstand any propaganda or omnipresence of Chinese troops or governmental figures. The international community accepts that Tibet is part of China but fails to mount any pressure on them, despite concrete evidence of human rights violations. There is an urgent need to create an area or embassy that would give Tibetans and others an outlet for assistance, without any threat to Beijing of galvanizing nationalist support. It is crucial to seek a power-sharing solution between the TGIE and Beijing to incorporate, within this structure, an embassy in Lhasa and other epicenter's such as Ngaba Prefecture. This solution requires an amalgamation of UN member states, both developing and developed, to bring about a venue and forum to assuage China's xenophobic fears of feeling "strong-armed" by states that they may feel are fearful of China's growing economic and military

Publishing, 2008, 160-161.

[85] embassy.goabroad.com/embassies-in/tibet. "Foreign Embassies and Consulates in Tibet." 16 March 2014. 16 March 2014. <http:embassy.goabroad.com/embassies-in/tibet.> Contact information is: Nepalese Consulate in Lhasa, Tibet. Consulate General of Nepal, Norbulingka Road13, Lhasa, Peoples Republic of China. Phone:(+86-891) 22880/1, 36890. Fax: (+86-891) 33689.

strength. In particular, the most effective way to accomplish this is to lead by example. Countries that are soft on human rights abusers within their public sector or through private enterprise need to adopt new policies to showcase their intentions for reforms. The United States can take a momentous step in the right direction by amending the use of capital punishment, taking a hard stance on gun ownership and control, relaxing the sanctions on Cuba that are having a deleterious effect on its citizens, and improving labour laws and the minimum wage for Americans.

Willingness from both Democrats and Republicans in Congress is needed to challenge the present structure in the U.S.; however, it gives current President Obama an opportunity to thrust America back into the "good graces" of the International Community after years of dismay over Former President Bush's unilateral foreign policy regarding the war in Iraq. Russia can also sow the seeds of reform by easing the current strife in Ukraine, extend the moratorium on capital punishment and bring it into the constitution, while limiting censure of the media, and holding transparent elections. The creation of a UN buffer zone within Lhasa or even on various border points can help diffuse conflict, constrain illegal transfer of goods and people across borders, while inculcating Chinese officials into the planning, creation and operation to ensure compliance among all parties. Canada can play a pivotal role in this operation where results can be measured. The absence of Chinese action and or interest in any reforms can be used as a linchpin to employ trade sanctions, tighter limits on FDI, and for other countries to expand trade with the European Union, Mercosur, Asean, NAFTA, ATO (African Trade Office), and other regional trade associations. Moreover, the institution of a product boycott of Chinese goods, while autarchic, seems to be the only plausible mechanism within the grasp of ordinary citizens to pressure the PRC into looking at the

Tibet situation through another lens, if a democratic solution is untenable. Corresponding

through written exchange with Heads of State is another egalitarian measure that may

increase awareness of the situation. Lastly, mobilising awareness through on-line

petitions provides another avenue.

Epilogue

Since the Chinese invasion of Tibet in 1949, China has declared sovereignty over Tibet through media and diplomatic channels. As evidence indicates, Tibet was independent economically, politically, and militarily despite periods where a patron-priest relationship existed with Mongolia, and Britain.

The Tibet question can be seen as a matter of conjecture due to the absence or lack of records giving a clear cut perspective on Chinese sovereignty over the region since Tibet's early period.

Racist tensions between Han Chinese and Tibetans is present, however it seems to be a factor that Beijing overlooked in their goal of modernising and expanding Tibet. Currently, despite ethnic Tibetans being the majority, they are increasingly left out of many governmental posts and senior positions. Furthermore, language is another tenuous issue with Mandarin being the primary language in post secondary schools. Tests for civil service positions are primarily held in Mandarin creating bitterness between the two groups. The adoption of fair testing and a bilingualism policy supported through a power-sharing arrangement may be the panacea for tensions in the region. Moreover, to stem unrest in the monastic community, limits need to be relaxed on the number of people entering monasteries to learn, practice, and teach Buddhism.

The Dalai Lama has been criticized for vacillating in his position over a one-country/two system approach. He has been without any real "bargaining chips" and would seem to be mellowing his approach with the passage of time as Beijing "digs in its heels." He has been steadfast in stating he wants a one-country/two system approach, particularly since the unrest in 2008. In view of the fact that the International Community sees Tibet as part of China, he has had to accept this position and has rightly moved away from his earlier stance on sovereignty for Tibet. The International Community can play a pivotal role to bring the two sides together to host talks leading to a power-sharing arrangement. As China grows stronger militarily and economically, the Tibet issue presents the possibility of a proxy division involving "soft power" to constrain Chinese authoritarianism on the Tibetan plateau. Tibetans and environmental groups need to focus more attention on the degradation of the bucolic landscape in order to preserve the balance of the delicate ecosystem, which has seen massive deforestation.

Adoption of a power-sharing arrangement need not mean the displacement of Han Chinese in the public sector, initially. The implementation of a balanced and fair political structure will ease ethnic tensions including cultural and religious freedom.

Initially, Beijing will need to maintain a small military base in Lhasa and on the perimeter to manage the huge border and utilize their skill to train Tibetans for a shared role in security. It will be expected that they will maintain this on a permanent basis.

The Dalai Lama is a high-profile figure that has created much visibility for the Tibet issue, angering the PRC, which considers this an internal matter. It would be a gambit for the Dalai Lama to restrict his movement and public appearances to soften the Chinese position towards him. On August 8, 2011 Dr. Lobsang Sangay was inaugurated as the democratically elected leader of the TGIE: the Kalon Tripa. In his speech he promised to return the Dalai Lama to Tibet and reached out to the Chinese people for compassion towards the goal of achieving a "Middle Way." As he travels extensively to meet foreign officials and foster support for the Tibetan cause, more martyrs adorn the list of those who have self-immolated.

List of Individuals Who Have Self – Immolated, Provided by 'The Tibet Bureau – Geneva.'

No	Name	Age	Monastery/Region	Father	Mother	Date of Self Immolation	Status
1	Tapey	20's				Feb.27.2009	unknown
2	Phuntsok Jarutsang	20	Kirti Monastery, Ngaba	Tsering Tashi	Dzongkar	March 3,2011	Died March 17, 2011
3	Tsewang Norbu/ Norko	29	Nyitso monastery, Tawn County	Tsokye	Choklek	August 15,2011	Died August 15,2011
4	Lobsang Kelsang	18-19	Kirti Monastery	Tsering Tashi		September 26,2011	unknown
5	Lobsang Kunchok	18-19	Kirti Monastery			September 26, 2011	unknown
6	Kelsang Wangchuk	17	Kirti Monastery	Tsurdri	Dechok	October 3, 2011	unknown
7	Choephel	19	formerly of Kirti Mon.			October 7, 2011	Died October 11, 2011
8	Khaying/Lhungyang	18	formerly of Kirti Mon.			October 7, 2011	Died October 8, 2011
9	Norbu Dramdul	19	formerly of Kirti Mon.			October 15, 2011	January 5, 2012
10	Tenzin Wangmo	20	Mamae Dechen Choekhorling Nunnery	Nyitse		October 17, 2011	October 17, 2011
11	Dawa Tsering	38	Karze monastery	Delek	Dontso	October 25, 2011	unknown
12	Palden Choesang/Choetso	35	Tawu Jangchup Choeling Nunnery	Joney	Kolen	November 3, 2011	November 3, 2011
13	Tenzin Phuntsok	46				December 1,	December

						2011	6, 2011
14	Ten-nyi	20	Kirti Monastery			January 6, 2012	January 6, 2012
15	Tsultrim	20	Ngaba			January 6, 2012	(D)January 7, 2012
16	Ven. Sonam Wangyal	42				January 8, 2012	(D) January 8, 2012
17	Lobsang Jamyang	22	Aduk Monastery, Ngaba	Gyatso	Lhachug	January 14, 2012	(D) January 14, 2012
18	Rikdzin Dorje(aka Ripke)	19	Me'uruma township, Ngaba	Garpa Tsongko	Dungkar	February 8, 2012	(D) February 21, 2012
19	Sonam Rabyang	42	Lab Monastery, Tridu, Kyegudo	Late Phuntsok Kyab	KunkyabWangmo	February 9, 2012	unknown
20	Tenzin Choedron	18	Mame Dechen Choekhorling Nunnery, Ngaba			February 11, 2012	(D) February 13, 2012
21	Lobsang Gyatso	19	Kirti Monastery	Badzri	Pelkar	February 13, 2012	unknown
22	Dhamchoe Sangpo	38	Bongthak Monastery	Late Takia Argutsang		February 17, 2012	(D) February 17, 2012
23	Nangdrol	18	Ngaba Zamthang Monastery	Chenzig	Nyingmo	February 19, 2012	(D) February 19, 2012
24	Tsering Kyi	20	Machu, student from middle school, Machu			March 3, 2012	(D) March 3, 2012
25	Rinchen	33	Ngaba			March 4, 2012	(D) March 4, 2012
26	Dorjee	18	Ngaba			March 5, 2012	(D) March 5, 2012
27	Gyepe	18	Kirti Monastery	Chakdor	Chaklo	March 10, 2012	(D) March 10, 2012

28	Jamyang Palden	34	Rongbo Gonchen Monastery, Rebkong			March 14, 2012	(D) September 29, 2012
29	Lobsang Tsultrim	20	Kirti Monastery	Yeshe	Tsedron	March 16, 2012	(D)March 19, 2012
30	Sonam Dhargye	43	Farmer; born in Sharlang, Nyen – tu-hu			March 17, 2012	(D) March 17, 2012
31	Sherab	20	Ngaba			March 28, 2012	(D) March 28, 2012
32	Tenpa Dhargyal	22	Gyalrong Tsodun Kirti Monastery, Ngaba	Kalden	Paltso	March 30, 2012	(D) April , 2012
33	Chime Palden	21	Gyalrong Tsodun Kirti Monastery, Ngaba	Rabgyal	Machik Tso	March 30, 2012	(D) March 30, 2012
34	Sonam	20's	Zamthang, Ngaba			April 19,2012	(D) April 19, 2012
35	Choepak Kyab	20's	Zamthang, Ngaba			April 19, 2012	(D) April 19, 2012
36	Dhargye(Thargyal)	20's	Lhasa			May 27, 2012	(D) July 7, 2012
37	Dorjee Tseten	19	Lhasa			May 27, 2012	(D)May 27, 2012
38	Rikyo	36	Zamthang, Ngaba	Chuklo	Rinlha	May 30, 2012	(D) May 30, 2012
39	Tamding Thar	50's	Chentsa, Amdo			June 15, 2012	(D) June 15, 2012
40	Ngawang Norpel	22	Zatoe Town, (Trindu, Jyekundo)	Lhakpa Dhondup	Tsering Yangchen	June 20, 2012	(D) August 1, 2012
41	Tenzin Khedup	24	Zatoe Town, (Trindu, Jyekundo)	Lekdup	Kyizom	June 20, 2012	(D) June 20, 2012
42	Dekyi Choezom	40's	Yushul			June 27, 2012	unknown
43	Tsewang Dorjee	22	Damshung, near			July 7, 2012	(D)July 10,

			Lhasa				2012
44	Lobsang Lozin	18	Ngaba,Gyalrong Tsodun Kirti Monastery	Jorgye	Tsepopo	July 17, 2012	(D) July 17, 2012
45	Lobsang Tsultrim	21	Kirti Monastery, Ngabo, Amdo	Tsewang	Donkar Kyi	August 6, 2012	(D) August 6, 2012
46	Dolkar Tso	26	Tsoe Tasar, Amdo	Druk Gyalkhar	Sangye Tso	August 7, 2012	(D) August 7, 2012
47	Choepa	24	Meuruma, Ngaba	Palho	Madon	August 10, 2012	(D) August 10, 2012
48	Lungtok	20	Kirti Monastery, Ngaba	Richung	Lumo	August 13, 2012	(D) August 13, 2012
49	Tashi	21	former monk at Kirti M., Ngaba		Ngapo	August 13, 2012	(D) August 14, 2012
50	Lobsang Kalsang	18	Kirti Monastery, Ngaba	Tsekho Dorjee	Sangaydon	August 27, 2012	(D) August 27, 2012
51	Dhamchoe	17	Ngaba	Doshi Lobe	Tsepo	August 27, 2012	(D) August 27, 2012
52	Yungdrung	27	Chamdo, Kham			September 29, 2012	unknown
53	Gudrup	43	Driru, Nagchu			October 4, 2012	(D) October 4, 2012
54	Sangay Gyatso	27	Tsoe, Kanlho	Gompo Dhondrup	Gompo Tso	October 6, 2012	(D) October 6, 2012
55	Tamdin Dorjee	52	Tsoe, Kanlho			October 13, 2012	(D) October 13, 2012
56	Lhamo Kyab	27	Bhora, Sangchu County, Kanlho			October 20, 2012	(D) October 20, 2012
57	Dhondup	n/a	Labrang, Sangchu County, Kanlho			October 22, 2012	(D) October 22, 2012
58	Dorjee Rinchen	57	Sangchu County, Kanlho			October 23, 2012	(D) October 23, 2012
59	Lhamo Tseten	24	Amchok, Sangchu County, Kanlho	Namchuk Tsering	Sungdue Tso	October 26, 2012	(D) October 26, 2012

60	Tsepag Kyab	21	Sangkhog		Lumo Jam	October 26, 2012	(D) October 26, 2012
61	Tsepo	20	Nagro Phampa, Driru, Nagchu TAR	Bhuchung	Gaga	October 25, 2012	(D) October 25, 2012
62	Tenzin	25	Nagro Phampa, Driru, Nagchu TAR	Nyima	Lugge	October 25, 2012	Unknown
63	Dorjee Lhundup	24	Rebgong, Amdo	Drukhar Gyal	Shawo Yakmo	November 4, 2012	(D) November 4, 2012
64	Dorjee	15	Ngaba	Tsering	Ghangkar	November 7, 2012	(D) November 7, 2012
65	Samdub	16	Ngaba	Sothar	Pasang	November 7, 2012	unknown
66	Dorjee Kyab	16	Ngaba	Tsering Dhondup		November 7, 2012	unknown
67	Tamdin Tso	23	Rebgong	Tamdin Kyab	Kunchok Tso	November 7,2012	(D) November 7, 2012
68	Unknown		Driru, Nagchu			November 7, 2012	unknown
69	Kalsang Jinpa	18	Rebgong	Choepa	Dechok Kyi	November 8, 2012	(D) November 8, 2012
70	Gonpo Tsering	19	Tsoe, Amdo	Tashi Sonam	Nyinglo	November 10, 2012	(D) November 10, 2012
71	Nyinkar Tashi	24	Rebgong			November 12, 2012	(D) November 12, 2012
72	Nyinchak Bum	18	Dowo, Rebgong			November 12, 2012	(D) November 12, 2012
73	Khabum Gyal	18	Gyalwo Luchungthang, Rebgong	Tadin Gyal	DolkarTso	November 15, 2012	(D) November 15, 2012
74	Tenzin Dolma	23	Goge village, Tsenmo	Bhulo	Tashi Dolma	November 15, 2012	(D) November 15, 2012

township,

Rebgong

75	Chagmo Kyi		Rebgong			November 17,2012	(D) November 17, 2012
76	Sangdhak Tsering	24	Dokar Township, Rebgong	Choeying	Menlha Tso	November 17, 2012	(D) November 17, 2012
77	Wangchen Norbu	25	Tsoshar, Amdo	Tenzin	Khando Tso	November 19, 2012	(D) November 19, 2012
78	Tsering Dhondup	34	Amchok	Lubum Gyal	Drukmo Tso	November 20, 2012	(D) November 20, 2012
79	Lubum Gyal	18	Dowa Town, Rebgong	Tsego		November 22, 2012	(D) November 22, 2012
80	Tadin Kyab	23	Luchu, Kanlho	Tsering Tashi (late)	Dolma Tso	November 22, 2012	(D) November 22, 2012
81	Tadin Dorjee	29	Tsekhog, Malho			November 23, 2012	(D) November 23, 2012
82	Wangyal	20's	Serthar			November 26, 2012	unknown
83	Sangay Dolma	17	Tsekhong, Malho	Sonam Gyal	Dhondup Tso	November 25, 2012	(D) November 25, 2012
84	Kunchok Tsering	18	Achok, Labrang	Tsephag Kyab	Gonpo Tso	November 26, 2012	(D) November 26,2012
85	Gonpo Tsering	24	Luchu, Kanlho	Wangyal	Namlolo	November 26, 2012	(D) November 26, 2012
86	Kalsang Kyab	24	Kyangtsa, Dzoege	Trogyal	Achoe	November 27, 2012	(D) November 27, 2012
87	Sangay Tashi	18	Sangchu, Labrang	Namkho		November 27, 2012	(D) November 27, 2012
88	Bendey Khar	21	Kanlho	Tsering Thar	Kunsang Dolma	November 28, 2012	(D) November 28, 2012
89	Tsering Namgyal	31	Luchu	Choero	Tamding Tso	November 29, 2012	(D) November 29, 2012
90	Kunchok	29	Zoegey,	Phuntsok	Lobsang	November	(D) November

	Kyab		Ngaba		Dolma	30, 2012	30, 2012
91	Sungdue Kyab	--	Bora, Labrang	Tsepa	Bendey Tso	December 2, 2012	unknown
92	Lobsang Gedun	29	Golog, Pema Dzong	Golog Lokho	Sago Dewang	December 3, 2012	(D) December 3, 2012
93	Kunchok Phelgye	24	Dzoege, Ngaba	Kunchok Kyab	Dolma Tso	December 8, 2012	(D) December 8, 2012
94	Pema Dorjee	23	Luchu			December 8, 2012	(D) December 8, 2012
95	Bhenchen Kyi	17	Tsekhog, Rebgong	Sonam Tsering	Sermo	December 9, 2012	(D) December 9, 2012
96	Tsering Tashi aka Tsebey	22	Sangchu, Kanlho	Dukar Kyab	Dolma Tsering	January 12, 2013	(D) January 12, 2013
97	Passang Lhamo	62	Beijing			September 13, 2012	unknown
98	Dupchok	28	Khyungchu, Ngaba	Kyokpo	Yangtso	January 18, 2013	(D) January 18, 2013
99	Kunchok Kyab	26	Bora, Ladang, Amdo	Dorjee	Rinchen Tso	January 22, 2013	(D) January 22, 2013
100	Lobsang Namgyal	37	Kirti Monastery	Karkho	Karkyi	February 3, 2013	(D) February 3, 2013
101	Drukpa Khar	26	Amchok, Sangchu County	Tamdin Tsering	Tamdin Tso	February 13, 2013	(D) February 13, 2013
102	Namlha Tsering	49	Sangchu, Kanlho			February 17, 2013	(D) February 17, 2013
103	Rinchen	17	Kyangtsa, Dzoge, Ngaba	Dhondup Tsering	Adon	February 19, 2013	(D) February 19, 2013
104	Sonam Dhargyal	18	Kyangsta, Dzoge, Ngaba	Tsering Dhondup	Takho	February 19, 2013	(D) February 19, 2013
105	Sangdak		Ngaba			February 25, 2013	unknown
106	Tsesung Kyab	20's	Kanlho			February 25, 2013	(D) February 25, 2013

107	Phagmo Dhondup	20's	Bayan Khar			February 24, 2013	NA
108	Kunchok Wangmo	30	Kirti Monastery, Ngaba		Depo	March 13, 2013	(D) March 13, 2013
109	Lobsang Thogmey	28	Kirti Monastery, Ngaba	Rogtrug	Depo	March 16, 2013	(D) March 16, 2013

The Tibet Bureau - Geneva indicates that 91 of 109 Tibetans have died from S.I., while the latest figures provided by 'Students For A Free Tibet' indicate that the number has risen to 127 as of February 2014. The principal reasons for S.I. are to generate awareness of Tibetan strife, foster freedom for Tibet, and allow for the return of the Dalai Lama.

Acknowledgements

It would be difficult to not mention the tremendous support during my academic career that I received from the University of Waterloo; in particular, Rose Padacz, Marianna Denes, Susan Shifflett, Katie Damphouse, Hank Edwards, and Henrietta Lemstra. Dr. Shiu Hing Sonny Lo, now at the Hong Kong Institute of Education, gave me creative license and positive support on this topic, and is sadly missed at Waterloo. Dr. Catia Grimani from the University of Urbino, Italy provided stellar friendship and research papers for me to proof, which helped to sharpen my focus. John & Julie Campbell of Kitchener were very supportive when my personal health was in recovery and my vehicles health was even worse; in fact, it had been the victim of a hit and run, mine was due to MS. Notable mention to my now – retired doctor of 35 years, belongs to Dr. Gary Houslander (Waterloo Ontario) for providing excellent health-care decisions, and deft administration. In addition, my son Christopher, who is a master of the Internet, provided resources to help bring this paper together in a workable format. Much knowledge and an improvement in health was gained along my journey through friend and healer, Susan Gross, Winterbourne, ON (1953-2010.) Eleanor F. Young, Rosseau, ON. (1919-2003) provided academic inspiration, and was a steadying influence. Leire Ramos Castro, Madrid, Spain is a very gifted artist that I was fortunate to connect with and who did the cover art for this work. Ironically, as we were working through this project, she indicated that she had traveled to Ladakh, India and was interested in and appreciative of Tibetan culture and Buddhism. I have included a few of her pictures that she had taken during her stay in Ladakh. Now, how is that for good karma!

GLOSSARY

Ambans - high official

Bodhisattva – layperson who through Buddhist practice, strives for awakening in order to help others

Boddhicitta – an awakened mind and heart that is totally dedicated for the benefit of others

Cohibio – confine, restrain, hold back, repress

Dharma – directory of teachings by the Buddha

Five Point Peace Plan – protocol for peace proposed by the Dalai Lama to China.
1.   Transformation of the whole of Tibet into a zone of peace;
2.   Abandonment of China's population transfer policy which threatens the very existence of the Tibetans as a people;
3.   Respect for the Tibetan people's fundamental human rights and democratic freedoms;
4.   Restoration and protection of Tibet's natural environment and the abandonment of China's use of Tibet for the production of nuclear weapons and dumping of nuclear waste;
5.   Commencement of earnest negotiations on the future status of Tibet and of relations between the Tibetan and Chinese peoples.

GINI Coefficient – a statistical measure of a nation-states income equality or inequality. Plotted on a 'Lorenz Curve'-) 0 represents total equality; 1 total inequality.

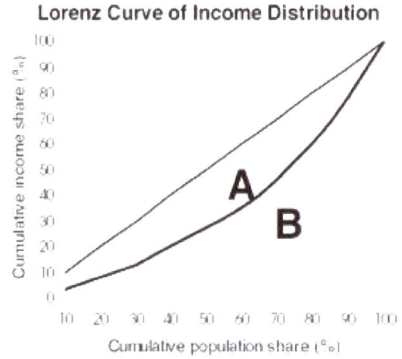

86

---

[86] Lorenz Chart used with kind permission from the World Bank. The World Bank is in no manner affiliated with the opinions expressed in this work.

Gradual Awakening – Mahayana school of Buddhism that propels individuals towards compassion and wisdom

Kalon Tripa – head of the Tibetan Government in Exile and leader of the Kashag (cabinet)

Modus Vivendi – an agreement that allows two individuals or groups to coexist peacefully until a formal decree can be attained

Panchen Lama – highest ranking next to the Dalai Lama; had acted as a 'regent' to the young Dalai Lama

Śākyamuni – Siddhārtha Gautama: the savant on whom Buddhist teachings were founded; the originator of Buddhism

Sangha – the Buddhist community including laity and ordained monks and nuns

70,000 Character Petition – the Panchen Lama proposed reforms to Chinese Premier Zhou Enlai in 1962, was declared an enemy of the people by Chairman Mao and exiled

1951 17 Point Agreement – a document signed between the Chinese and Tibetan governments that is claimed illegitimate by the Dalai Lama and Tibetans as it is claimed to be agreed to under duress

Sudden Awakening – Chinese Chan School or 'Zen' of Buddhist strictures; considered a proponent of Hinayana Buddhism

TAR – (Tibetan Autonomous Region) 2nd largest province within China, after Xinjiang

TGIE (Tibetan Government in Exile) – founded by the Dalai Lama in 1963; a new Constitution: 'Charter for Tibetans in Exile' was ratified in 1991

The Dalai Lama – Tenzin Gyatso, July 6, 1935. Founded the TGIE in Dharamsala, India after a failed coup against Chinese occupiers & spiritual leader.

TYC – (Tibetan Youth Council) – international NGO (Non-Governmental Organisation) that advocates Tibetan independence

---

web.worldbank.org
WBSITE/EXTERNAL/TOPICS/EXTPOVERTY/EXTPA/0,,contentMDK:20238991~menuPK:492138~pagePK:148956~piPK:216618~theSitePK:430367,00.html

Works Cited

Barboza, David. "660 Held in Tibetan Uprising, China Says." NYTimes.com. 27 March

2008. 2 August 2009

<http://www.nytimes.com/2008/03/27/world/asia/27tibet.html>.

Dagmar Bernstorff and Hubertus Von Welck. "An Interview with Tenzin Gyatso, the

Fourteenth Dalai Lama." Exile As Challenge The Tibetan Diaspora. New Delhi:

Orient Longman, 2004. 113-114.

Buncombe, Andrew. "Dalai Lama: I am prepared to face China. I will go to

Beijing."Independent.co.uk.com. 21 March 2008. 2 August 2009

<http://www.independent.co.uk/news/world/asia/dalai-lama-i-am-

prepared-to-face-china-i-will-go-to-beijing-798998.html>.

Bradsher, Keith. "China Slows Purchases of U.S. and Other Bonds." NYTimes.com. 12

April 2009. 1 August 2009

<http://www.nytimes.com/2009/04/13/business/global/13yuan.html>.

Brown, Kerry. "Obama, Xi, and the Dalai Lama: How to Address the Tibet Issue."

www.thediplomat.com. 04 March 2014. 08 March 2014.

<http://www.thediplomat.com/2014/03/obama-xi-and-the-dalai-lama-

how-to-address-the-tibet-issue/>.

Burr, William. "The Sino-Soviet Border Conflict, 1969: U.S. Reactions and Diplomatic

Maneuvers." 12 June 2001. 21 April 2014.
<http://www2.gwu.edu/~nsarchiv/NSAEBB/NSAEBB49/index2.html>.

Bush III, Richard. "Interview on Tibet." Post-Colonial Transformations in China's

Hong Kong & Macao: Implications for Cross-Taiwan Strait and Canada-PRC

Links Conference. University of Waterloo, Waterloo. 27 June 2009.

CBC News. France Ponders Boycott OF Beijing Over Tibet Conflict.

CBCNEWS.ca. 18 March 2008. 4 August 2009

"China's Defense Budget." GlobalSecurity.org. 20 April 2009. 2 August 2009

<http://www.globalsecurity.org/military/world/china/budget.htm>.

The Economic Times. "China, Russia settle border dispute." 15 October 2004. 21

April 2014. < http://articles.economictimes.indiatimes.com/2004-10-

15/news/27395578_1_russia-and-china-diplomatic-ties-tarabarov>.

Goldstein, Melvyn C. The Snow Lion And The Dragon. London: University of

California Press, 1997.

Eva Herzer and Sara B. Levin. "China's Denial Of Tibetan Women's Right To

Reproductive Freedom." October 10, 1995. April 20, 2014.

<http://www.tibetjustice.org/reports/women/chinas_denial.html>.

His Holiness the Dalai Lama. "Five Point Peace Plan for Tibet."

http://www.dalailama.com/messages/tibet/five-point-peace-plan. 22 April

2014 <http://www.tibet.com/proposal/5point.html>.

Lieberthal, Kenneth. Governing China From Revolution Through Reform. New York:

W.W. Norton & Co., 2004.

International Campaign For Tibet. Website Content Producer, Morgan Riehl.9 April

2014.<http://www.savetibet.org/wpcontent/uploads/2013/06/ICT_politica

l_prisoner_list_full.pdf >.

International Campaign For Tibet. Jampa: The Story Of Racism In Tibet.September

2001. 16 August 2009. USA: ICT, 26. < http://www.savetibet.org/wpcontent/uploads/2013/01/JampaRacism.pdf >.

International Campaign for Tibet. "Self-Immolations by Tibetans." 17 February

2014. 13 March 2014. < http://www.savetibet.org/resources/fact-

sheets/self-immolations-by-tibetans/>.

Lowe, Christian. "Expansive China faces grass roots resentment." Reuters 18 August

2009. 18 August 2009

<http://www.reuters.com/article/ousiv/idUSTRE57H00220090818>.

Lopez, Donald S. The Madman's Middle Way. Chicago and London: The University of

Chicago Press, 2006.

Mann, R.S. Ladakh Then And Now. New Delhi: Mittal Publications. 2002.

Martina Michael and Greg Torode. "China's Xi ramps up military spending in face of

worried region." www.reuters.com. 5 March 2014. 7 March 2014.

< www.reuters.com/article/2014/03/05/us-china-parliament-defence-

idUSBREA2403L20140305.>

Minority Rights Group International, World Directory of Minorities and

Indigenous Peoples-China: Tibetans, July 2008. 31 July 2009.

< http://www.unhcr.org/cgi-

bin/texis/vtx/refworld/rwmain?page=printdoc&docid=49749d3dc>.

Narveson, Jan. "Have We A Right To Non-Discrimination?"Business Ethics In Canada.

Ed. Poff, Deborah C. and Wilfred J. Waluchow. Scarborough: Prentice-Hall,
1991.

Page, Jeremy. "Dalai Lama Offers His Flock A Vote On Whether He Should Be Re-

incarnated." The Times 28 November 2007. 7 June 2009

<http://www.timesonline.co.uk/tol/comment/faith/article2955350.ece?tok
en=null&offset=0&page=1>.

Pei, Minxin. China's Trapped Transition: The Limits of Developmental Autocracy.
Cambridge: Harvard University Press, 2006.

Powers, John. Introduction to Tibetan Buddhism. New York: Snow Lion Publications,
2007.

Prathibha, MS. "China's 2014 Defence Budget: An Assessment." IDSA. 21 April 2014.
21 April 2014.
<http://www.idsa.in/idsacomments/Chinas2014DefenceBudget_msprathibh
a_210414>.

Raddatz, Martha and Jenna Mucha. "Clinton Seeks To Reassure China On T-Bills."
ABC News.go.com. 21 February 2009. 1 August 2009
<http://abcnews.go.com/International/story?id=6930021&page=1>.

Rapoza, Kenneth. "The China Miracle: A Rising Wealth Gap." Forbes January 20,
2013. April 20, 2014. <
http://www.forbes.com/sites/kenrapoza/2013/01/20/the-china-miracle-a-
rising-wealth-gap/>.

refworld "World Directory of Minorities and Indigenous Peoples-China:
Tibetans."July 2008. 21 April 2014.
< http://www.refworld.org/docid/49749d3dc.html
http://www.unhcr.org/cgibin/texis/vtx/refworld/rwmain?page=printdoc&
amp;docid=49749d3dc>.

Richardson, Hugh. Tibet and Its History. London: Oxford University Press, 1962.

Roberts, John B and Elizabeth Roberts. Freeing Tibet. New York: AMACOM. 2009.

Sautman, Barry. Colonialism, Genocide, and Tibet. London: Routledge. 2006.

Sautman Barry. "Protests in Tibet and Separatism: the Olympics and Beyond."

Permanent Mission of the People's Republic of China to the UN. 16 April

2008. 3 August 2009

<http://www.mfa.gov.cn/ce/ceun/eng/gyzg/xizang/t425983.htm>.

Smith Jr, Warren W. China's Tibet. Lanham: Rowman & Littlefield Publishers,

2008.

Starmass.com. 2012. 21 April 2014. < http://www.starmass.com/china-

review/imports-exports/china-top-export-market.htm>.

Stein, R.A. Tibetan Civilisation. Stanford: Stanford University Press, 1972.

TCHRD.com 2007.Tibet Centre For Human Rights and Democracy. 16 May 2009

<http://www.tchrd.org/publications/annual_reports/2007/ar_2007.pdf>.

Shakya, Tershing. The Dragon In The Land of Snows. New York: Columbia University

Press, 1999.

Thonsur, Tsering Norzom. "Women: Emancipation in Exile." Exile As Challenge The

Tibetan Diaspora. New Delhi: Orient Longman, 2004. 323.

Thurman, Robert. Why The Dalai Lama Matters. New York: Beyond Words
Publishing, 2008.

The Tibet Bureau-Genf. 20 March 2013. 2 April 2014.

<www.tibetoffice.ch/selfimmolations/>.

Tse-tung, Mao. "On The Policies For Our Work In Tibet—Directive Of The Central

Committee Of The Communist Party Of China". From The Selected Works Of

Mao Tse-tung. Foreign Languages Press. Vol V, 1977, pp. 73-76. July 4, 2009.

    <http://www.marx2mao.com/Mao/WT52.html>.

United Nations Development Programme. Human Development Report 2013.

    Director and Lead Author, Khalid Malik. 2013. April 15 2014.

    <http://hdr.undp.org/sites/default/files/reports/14/hdr2013_en_complete.

    pdf>.

Yao, Wang. "Hu Yaobang's Visit To Tibet, May 22–31, 1980. An important

    Development In The Chinese Government's Tibet Policy." Resistance And

    Reform In Tibet. Ed. Robert Barnett and Shirin Akiner. Bloomington and

    Indianapolis: Indiana University Press, 1994.

Wikipedia. "Religion in China; 3.1 Statistics." 15 March 2014. 20 March 2014.

    <http://www.en.wikipedia.org/wiki/Religion_in_China.>

Wong, Edward. "China's Money and Migrants Pour Into Tibet." New York Times. 24

    July 2010. 23 April 2014.

    <http://www.nytimes.com/2010/07/25/world/asia/25tibet.html?pagewan

    ted=all&_r=0>.

The World Bank. "GDP Ranking." 2012. 7 March 2014.

    <http://databank.worldbank.org/data/download/GDP.pdf >.

INDEX

A

ambans. *See* political authority
Avalokitesvara
     Three Kings, *1*

B

Barry Sautman. *See* LA riots 1992
Blue Annals. *See* White Annals
boycott, 2

C

cadres. *See* discrimination in state sector
Chiang Kai-shek. *See* autonomy
China second globally in GDP as of 2012, 37
Chinese Chan School. *See* sudden awakening
civil disobedience. *See* 80,000 incidents
corruption, vii, 4, 30

D

Dharamsala. *See* Dalai Lama

E

European Union. *See* solutions

F

FDI (Foreign Direct Investment). *See* China's
     economy
Five Point Peace Plan. *See* Dalai Lama 5 Point Peace
     Plan
forced abortions, 27, 33

G

GINI coefficient. *See* explanation of China's
     performance
Glasnost, 30
Great Leap Forward, 19
Great Tibet. *See* treaty

H

Han Chinese. See Tibet, economy , See Tibet,
     economy , See Tibet, economy , See Tibet,
     economy , See Tibet, economy , See Tibet,
     economy , See Tibet, economy , See Tibet,
     economy , See Tibet, economy , See Tibet,
     economy , See Tibet, economy , See Tibet,
     economy , See Tibet, economy , See Tibet,
     economy , See Tibet, economy , See Tibet,
     economy , See Tibet, economy , See Tibet,

economy , See Tibet, economy , See Tibet, economy ,
     See Tibet, economy , See Tibet, economy
Heshang Moheyan. *See* debate
Hu Jintao. *See* Dalai Lama negotiations

I

International Community, 2, 4, 31, 34

J

John Powers, 5

K

Kamala´sîla. *See* debate

L

Ladakh, 12, 15, 32, 33, 55, 60
Leire Ramos Castro, 15, 55
Lhabsang Khan. *See* Dzungar
List of Individuals Who Have Self – Immolated. *See*
     The Tibet Bureau - Geneva

M

Mahayana. *See* awakening
Mao Tse-tung. See Mao Zedong, Chairman Mao, See
     Mao Zedong, Chairman Mao, See Mao Zedong,
     Chairman Mao, See Mao Zedong, Chairman Mao
Mao Zedong, vi
March 10. *See* anniversary of failed uprising
Middle Way. *See* Dalai Lama
Minxin Pei. *See* China's chances for
     Democratisation
modus vivendi. *See* China, Tibet

N

Narveson, Jan. *See* discrimination
Nepalese Consulate in Lhasa, Tibet, 42
NGO. *See* UNICEF
Nobel peace prize. See Dalai Lama, See Dalai Lama

P

Panchen Lama, 2, 10, 12, 18, 19, 20, 21, 22, 57
patron-priest relationship. *See* Mongols, Tibet
PCTAR. *See* Preparatory Committee for the Tibet
     Autonomous Region
People's Liberation Army. See PLA, See PLA
Perestroika, 30
Potala, *1*

About the Author

Kevin Kieswetter resides in Waterloo, Ontario, Canada. He graduated from the University of Waterloo, majoring in Political Science and minoring in International Studies. Through a connection with Buddhism, he has found positive healing results to manage MS. As part of his fitness regimen he cycles, swims, and has regular workouts. For enjoyment purposes, music is a great source, as are the Miami Dolphins and Montreal Canadiens sports teams. As a political junkie, he sees his concern for Tibet and Tibetans expressed through his written work.

www.ingramcontent.com/pod-product-compliance
Lightning Source LLC
Chambersburg PA
CBHW061050290526
45796CB00002B/8